THE COUNTRY ROCK GUITAR BOOK

Discover Authentic Country Rock Techniques, Riffs and Licks

STUART RYAN

FUNDAMENTAL CHANGES

The Country Rock Guitar Book

Discover Authentic Country Rock Techniques, Riffs and Licks

ISBN: 978-1-78933-415-9

Published by www.fundamental-changes.com

Copyright © 2023 Stuart Ryan

Edited by Tim Pettingale

The moral right of this author has been asserted.

All rights reserved. No part of this publication may be reproduced, stored in a retrieval system, or transmitted in any form or by any means, without the prior permission in writing from the publisher.

The publisher is not responsible for websites (or their content) that are not owned by the publisher.

www.fundamental-changes.com

For over 350 free guitar lessons with videos check out:

www.fundamental-changes.com

Join our free Facebook Community of Cool Musicians

www.facebook.com/groups/fundamentalguitar

Tag us for a share on Instagram: **FundamentalChanges**

Cover Image Copyright: Shutterstock, iraua

Contents

Introduction 4

Get the Audio 5

Chapter One – Overview of Country Picking Techniques 6
    Crosspicking 6
    Fingerpicking 11
    Hybrid Picking 13

Chapter Two – An Introduction to String Bending 18

Chapter Three – String Bending Licks 28

Chapter Four – Harmonised Guitar Parts 34

Chapter Five – Artist Studies 1 47
    Allen Collins 47
    Ed King 49
    Gary Rossington 51
    Duane Allman 53
    Dickey Betts 54

Chapter Six – Artist Studies 2 57
    Buffalo Springfield/The Byrds 57
    Joe Walsh 59
    Don Felder 61
    Glenn Frey 65
    Bernie Leadon 67
    John Fogerty 71
    Keith Richards and Mick Taylor 73

Chapter Seven – Performance Pieces 76
    Performance piece 1 76
    Performance piece 2 80
    Performance piece 3 84
    Performance piece 4 89

Conclusion 94

Introduction

There are times in music when styles collide to create something new and ahead of its time. In the late 1960s, musicians began to explore what would happen if they mixed the traditional sounds of country music with the harder sounds of the burgeoning rock scene.

Across the west coast of America, bands like The Byrds and Buffalo Springfield searched for a new sound, where traditional instrumentation was married with the more modern sound of the electric guitar. This paved the way for bands like The Eagles, Creedence Clearwater Revival, and many more, who would take this sound and add to it the harder edge of 1970s rock.

Meanwhile, another variety of country rock was developing in the southern states, as legendary groups The Allman Brothers and Lynyrd Skynyrd created a tougher sound than the Laurel Canyon bands of L.A. In the U.K., The Rolling Stones refined their "honky-tonk" country sound into a more aggressive country rock and yet another subset of the genre emerged.

Just as the 1960s had seen the birth of the guitar hero, the 1970s saw the further development of the guitarist as a virtuoso. Guitar solos became longer, extravagant harmony guitar licks came to the fore, and the age of the riff had truly arrived. All of this added to the development of the country rock sound.

In this book, you'll discover how the legends of country rock guitar made the style their own – artists, such as Joe Walsh, Duane Allman, Don Felder, Allen Collins and many more. You'll learn how instruments like the banjo and Dobro shaped the sound of these players, and you'll explore the techniques and language you need to master this style.

You'll also discover how the radio friendly sounds of L.A. country rock contrast with the harder swagger of the southern sound. Finally, you'll put it all into practice with artist studies, accompanied by authentic sounding full tracks, where rhythm and lead combine.

So, let's get started on your journey into the world of country rock guitar!

Get the Audio

The audio files for this book are available to download for free from **www.fundamental-changes.com.** The link is in the top right-hand corner. Simply select this book title from the drop-down menu and follow the instructions to get the audio.

We recommend that you download the files directly to your computer, not to your tablet, and extract them there before adding them to your media library. You can then put them on your tablet or smart phone. On the download page, there is a help PDF, and we also provide technical support via the contact form.

For over 350 free guitar lessons with videos check out:

www.fundamental-changes.com

Join our free Facebook Community of Motivated Musicians

www.facebook.com/groups/fundamentalguitar

Tag us for a share on Instagram: **FundamentalChanges**

Chapter One – Overview of Country Picking Techniques

Country rock guitar features various approaches to picking technique, since it fuses together the styles of country and rock. In order to play this style of music in an authentic manner, you'll need to have an appreciation of the three main approaches: cross picking, fingerpicking and hybrid picking.

Crosspicking uses the pick to play across the strings, fingerpicking uses only the fingers, and hybrid picking uses a combination of pick and fingers to achieve a similar but different effect.

Each technique could easily warrant an entire book in its own right, so consider this chapter a primer. It will give you the opportunity to try each approach and see which one suits you best. After studying this chapter, you'll know how to practice these techniques and how to incorporate them into your playing.

Country rock players draw influence from the banjo, dobro and lap steel, seeking to replicate those sounds on a regular guitar. The picking approaches we'll examine are used to mimic the wider intervallic jumps commonly found on these instruments.

A technique such as hybrid picking might require you to adapt and develop things you already know, or it may be completely new to you. With all of these picking approaches, take the exercises slowly at first, and concentrate on putting a firm technical foundation in place. If one particular approach really appeals to you, there is plenty of learning material available to further your skills, and Fundamental Changes publish a number of books dedicated to picking techniques.

Crosspicking

Crosspicking is a bluegrass accompaniment technique that has found its way into country rock. Listen to the intro to *Sweet Home Alabama* and you'll hear crosspicking in action. At its heart, crosspicking means to use the pick to play arpeggios within chord shapes, and this typically means a combination of picking adjacent strings and jumping across strings. Crosspicking allows you to move from low to high strings and vice versa, just as a fingerpicker would, but with the tone produced by the attack of a pick.

The difficulty of this technique depends on the distance we need to jump across the strings. Picking adjacent strings cleanly at speed can be hard enough, but jumping from, say, the A string across to the B or high E string is typical in country rock and demands a loose wrist action combined with accurate picking. Then we have to factor in playing more challenging rhythms. So, the following exercises begin with a basic crosspicking approach, then gradually become more complex.

Example 1a is a crosspicking part played on an open D Major chord. Play it with the following picking pattern: a downstroke on the D string, downstroke on the G string, upstroke on the B string, and another upstroke on the G string.

That covers the first four notes. You'll repeat this pattern through the sequence, but the challenge is to move between the other bass notes (on the A string and low E strings) while keeping the picking clean and accurate. It's good training for moving between bass notes on adjacent strings.

Example 1a

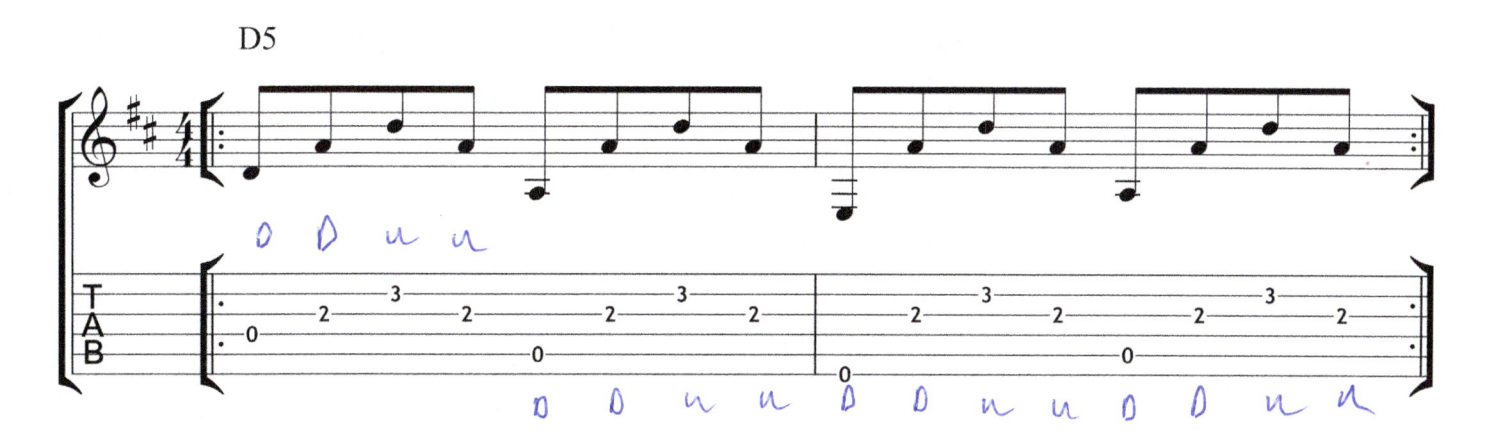

[Musical notation and tablature for Example 1a, in D5, showing picking pattern markings D D u u repeated]

In the next example, the fretting hand needs to change its grip to play the part, so there's more to think about, however picking pattern is the same as the previous example.

The third finger stays fretted on the B string throughout. The second finger will move across to hold down the 3rd fret of the A string, but then you need to switch to the first finger to hold down the note at the 2nd fret.

Once you've got the picking pattern and movements down, use a metronome to help you build up speed. Increase the tempo until playing this becomes a challenge and you'll gradually be able to increase the pace over time.

Example 1b

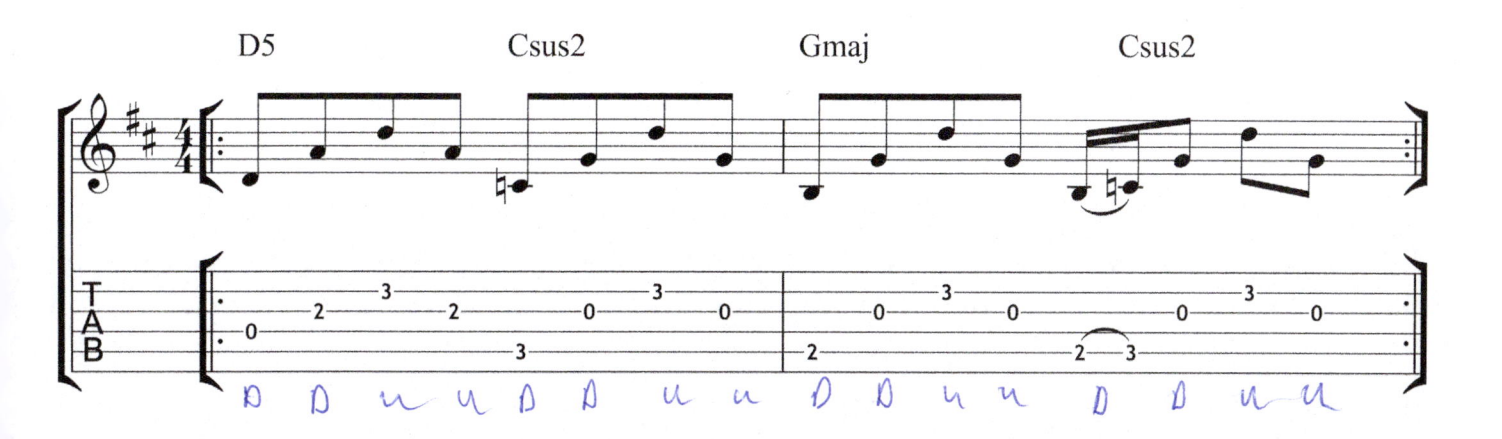

[Musical notation and tablature for Example 1b, with chords D5, Csus2, Gmaj, Csus2, showing picking pattern markings D D u u repeated]

The fretting hand moves in the same way in the next example, but here the crosspicking rhythm is more complex and the pick is targeting different strings. There is a bit of jumping around in this exercise and the tricky rhythms demand a loose, accurate picking hand.

In bar one, start by playing downstrokes on the D and G strings, followed by upstrokes on the E, B and G strings. When you get to beat 3 in the second bar (A string, 3rd fret) use two downstrokes, followed by a downstroke for the combined notes on the G and B strings.

Example 1c

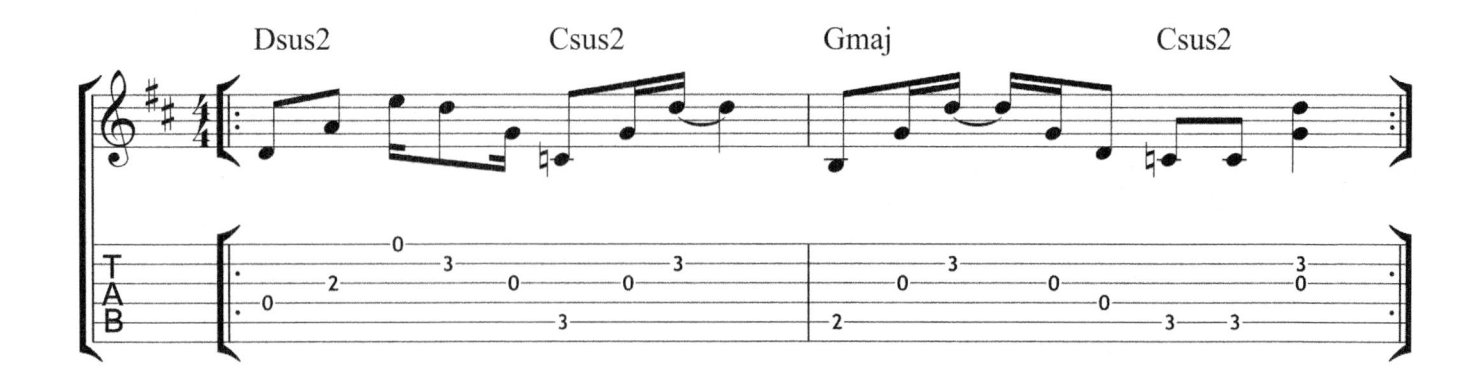

[Musical notation and tablature showing chords: Dsus2, Csus2, Gmaj, Csus2]

The following riff is inspired by Lynyrd Skynyrd and has a lot more movement, as it includes some embellishments.

The idea begins with two downstrokes on the A string, followed by upstrokes on the B, G and D strings. As you pick upward on the G string, pull off from the 2nd fret to the open G with your first finger.

Bar two begins with a hammer-on from the open A string to the 2nd fret, executed with the first finger, while the third finger holds down the 3rd fret of the B string. Next, use the second finger to play the C bass note on the A string, 3rd fret, while the first finger moves across a string to play the hammer-on/pull-off embellishments on the D string.

Work through the whole idea slowly to begin with, as there are a lot of moving parts. Listen to the audio and you'll hear that the strings are allowed to ring after being plucked – especially the high strings – so be sure not to accidentally mute them when playing.

Example 1d

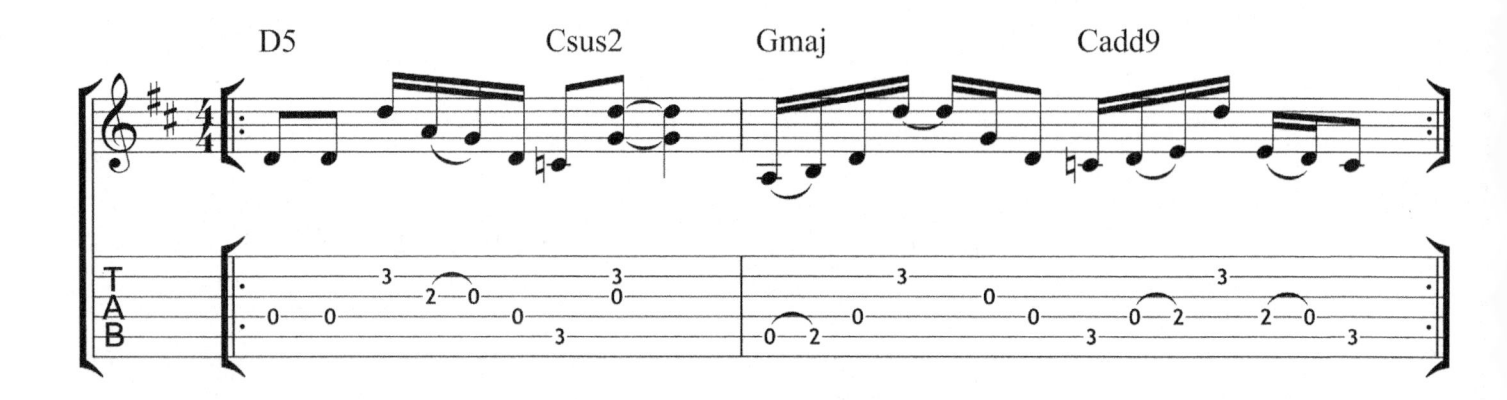

[Musical notation and tablature showing chords: D5, Csus2, Gmaj, Cadd9]

This example increases the pace to emulate the sound of a banjo picker. Don't be put off by this – as with all these examples, the important thing is to work out the fingering, practice the picking movements, and to do it all slowly, to drill it into muscle memory. Speed can come later.

When I'm playing patterns like this I'll aim for downstrokes across the strings until I reach the last note before the sequence reverses. In this example, I'd start with three downstrokes over the A, D and G strings followed by upstrokes on the B and G strings, the play a downstroke on the D string and an upstroke on the G before moving to the FMaj7 chord.

Example 1e

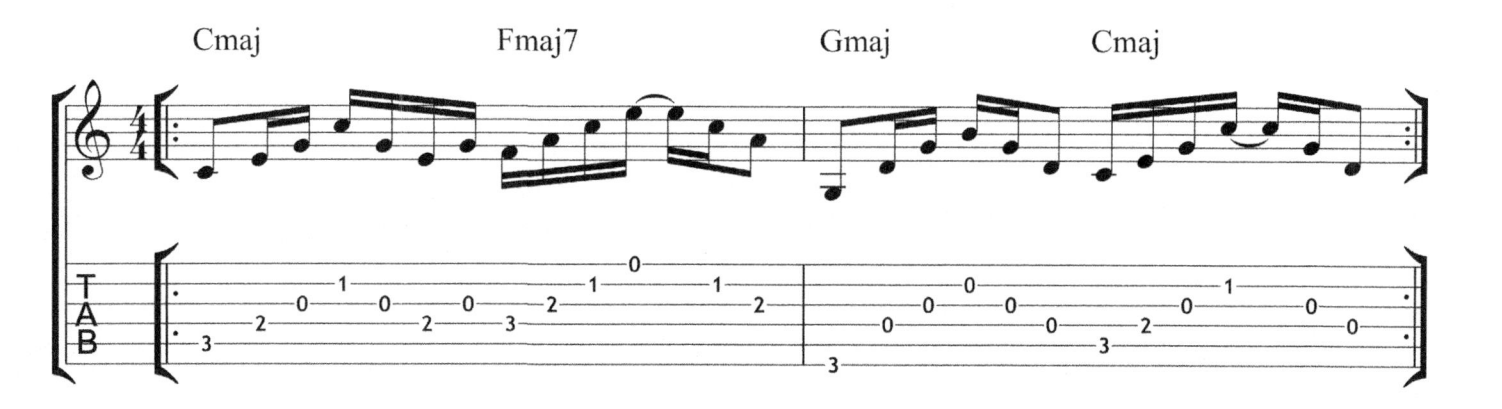

Adding hammer-on embellishments within a chord shape is what gives us the authentic Bluegrass accompaniment sound. Using hammer-ons also means there is less work for the pick to do – it's just a matter of coordination and practice to bring it all together.

This example requires some deft re-fingering to move between the C and F chords in bar one. Begin by holding down a regular open C chord. The hammer-on from the open D string will be played by the second finger. Play the A and D strings with downstrokes. Now play the B, G, and D strings with upstrokes. As you transition from the C to F chord, play the D string 3rd fret with the third finger. You second finger will then hop over to the G string to execute the pull-off from fret 2 to the open string.

In bar two, begin with what looks like a standard open C chord, but with the bass note relocated to the low E string, 3rd fret. Hold this shape throughout bar two. The picking pattern is the same for both bars.

Example 1f

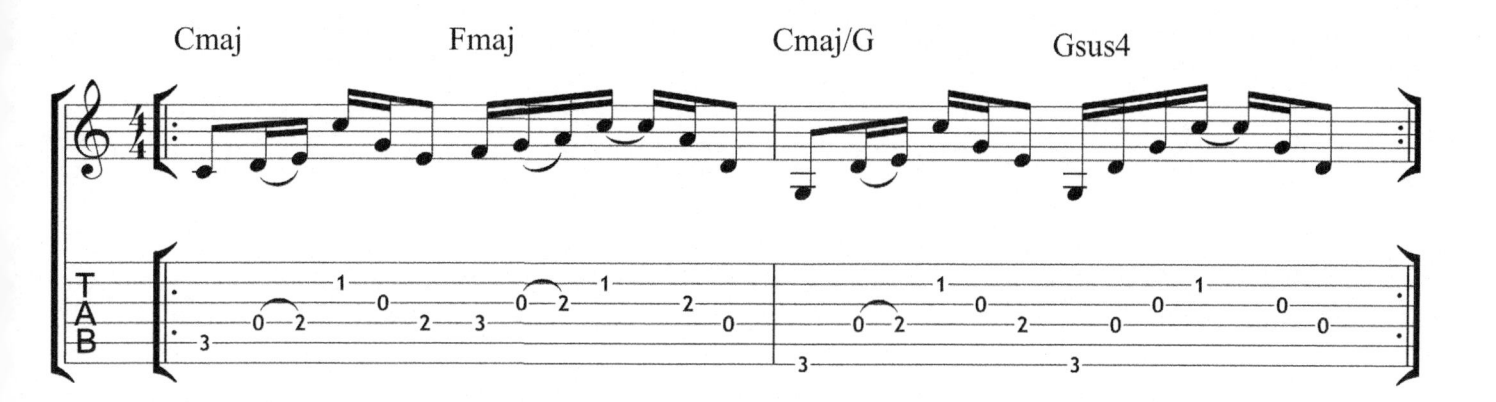

Playing triads – simple three note major and minor chords – on the top three strings is another great way to emulate the approach of a banjo player.

Playing over three adjacent strings also means the picking pattern can often remain the same throughout. Play this idea with downstrokes for the G and B strings, followed by upstrokes for the E and B strings, then a downstroke on the G string. The picking pattern is similar for the rest of the lick.

Example 1g

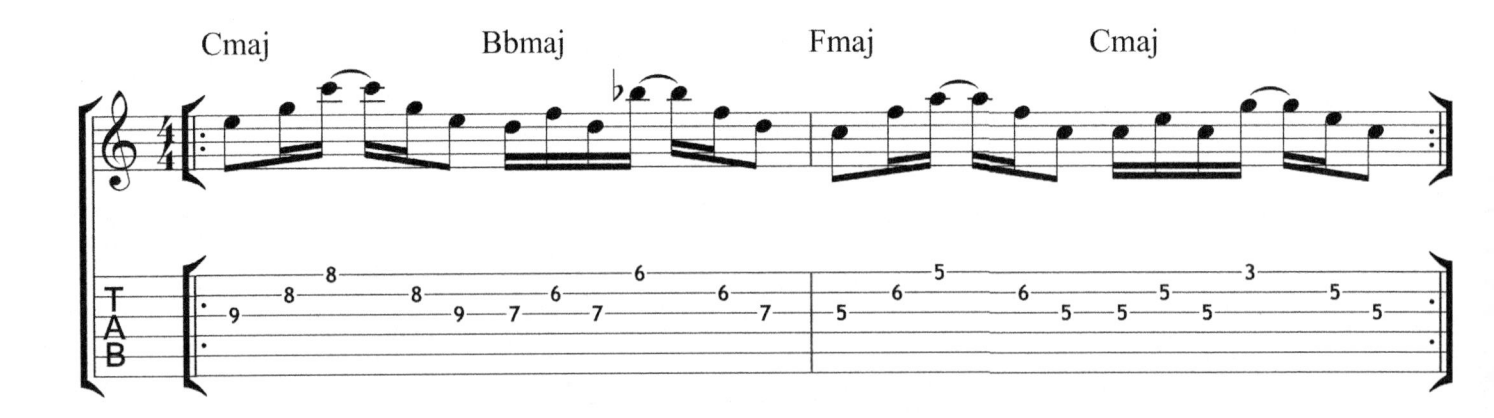

Crosspicking patterns like the intro to The Eagles *Hotel California* often have melodic content, which can mean more rhythms are combined in the sequence. This example contrasts a brisker feel on beats 1 and 2 with more space on beats 3 and 4. Try practicing this one with a metronome set to approximately 80bpm to see if you can control the picking hand over these different rhythms.

Example 1h

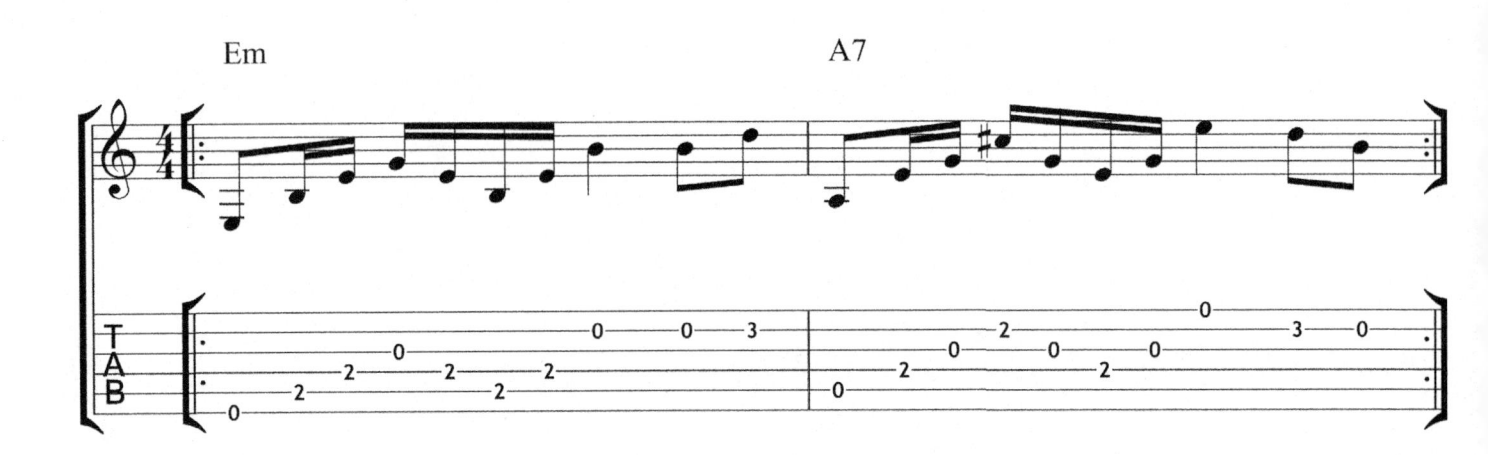

Fingerpicking

Country rock artists like Jackson Browne and James Taylor play almost exclusively fingerstyle, so this is a technique you should definitely be familiar with. As mentioned, this is far too large a topic to get into in detail, but here is a brief introduction to the main fingerpicking approaches relevant to the country rock style.

Like the hybrid picking approach that will follow, one of the strengths of fingerpicking is to pluck strings over wider intervals, and to be able to sound strings simultaneously. Fingerpicking also lends itself to building "rolling" patterns across the strings, much like a banjo player.

If you are new to fingerstyle, the main difficulty can be "what goes where" in terms of the picking fingers. To begin with, the easiest approach is to use the thumb to play the low E, A and D strings (which most of the time will be the bass notes) the first finger for the G string, the second finger for the B string, and the third finger for the high E string.

Here's a simple plucked idea where the notes sound simultaneously. It includes a typical Jackson Browne style descending bassline.

Example 1i

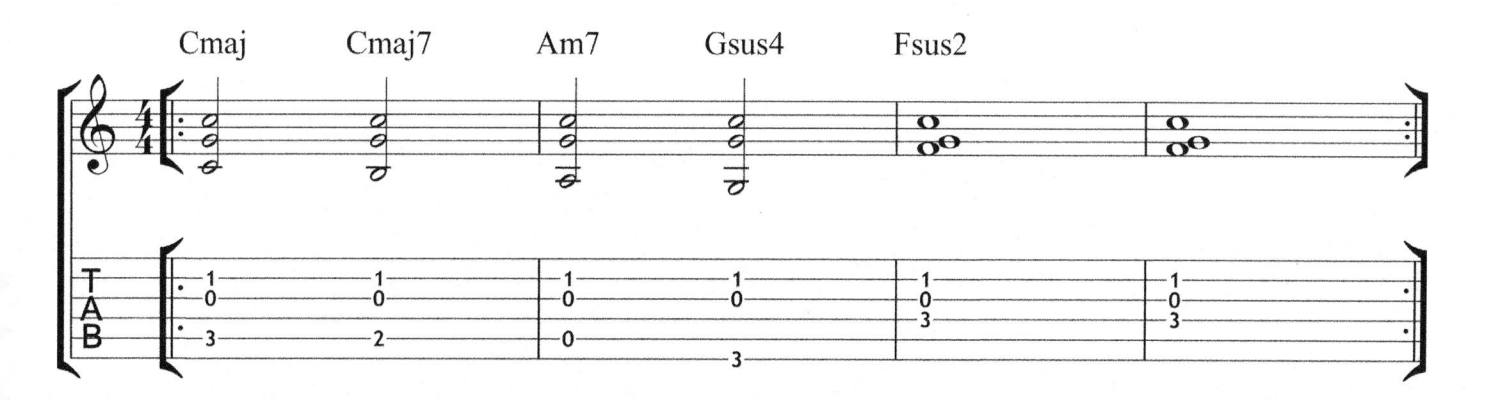

Rolling patterns across the strings is the classic fingerstyle sound. This approach makes the descending bassline stand out much more prominently. Pluck downward with the thumb to sound the bass notes, and upward with the first and second fingers to sound the notes on the B and G strings. Work at getting a smooth, consistent timing between your thumb and fingers, so that all notes are played with an even volume and in time.

In the fretting hand, the first finger will remain at the 1st fret of the B string throughout, while the bassline moves around it. Use the third finger for bass notes at the 3rd fret and second finger for bass notes at the 2nd fret.

Example 1j

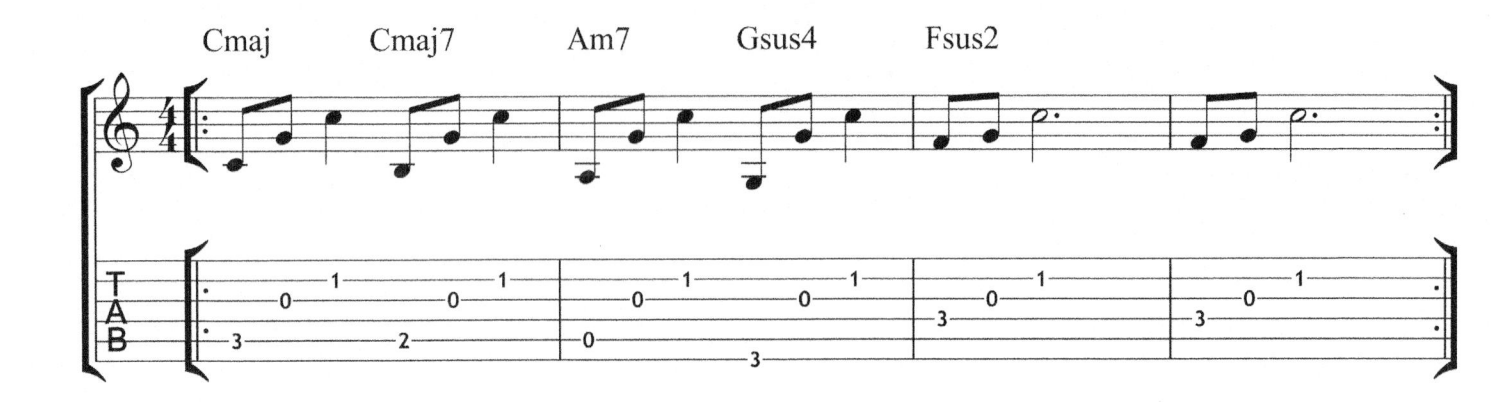

Fingerpicking patterns often have a *forward-back* approach to sounding the strings. In other words, the thumb rolls down the strings, and the fingers pluck back up them.

Here, the thumb plays the notes on strings six, five and four, while the second and first fingers pluck the B and G strings respectively.

Example 1k

Fingerpicking lets you play strings that are far away from each other. In this example, start off with the thumb plucking the A string and the index finger sounding the B string. Make a pinching motion with thumb and finger to sound strings simultaneously and aim to get an even volume between both.

Example 1l

[Musical notation and tablature showing chords: Cmaj, Cmaj7, Am7, C/G, Fsus2]

Hybrid Picking

As an alternative to fingerstyle, country rock guitarists will often use *hybrid picking* to replicate the sounds of the banjo, pedal steel and Dobro. Hybrid picking is useful for playing similar ideas to fingerstyle, but the inclusion of the pick allows for more attack, compared to the softer sound of fingerstyle. It's also a useful technique to have under your belt for when you want to switch seamlessly between playing picking patterns and soloing normally with the pick.

There are essentially two approaches to playing hybrid. In each version, the pick is gripped between the thumb and first finger, and different combinations of the remaining free fingers are used for plucking strings.

The first type of hybrid picking uses the plectrum and the second finger only to pick the notes. In this style, the picking hand will glide across the strings and lines will be played with a pinching motion, with the pick playing all downstrokes and the second finger plucking all upstrokes.

In this first example, use the plectrum to pick the G string and the second finger to pluck the high E string. You could, of course, play this like with the pick alone, but I want you to notice how using hybrid technique means you don't have to jump across any strings.

Example 1m

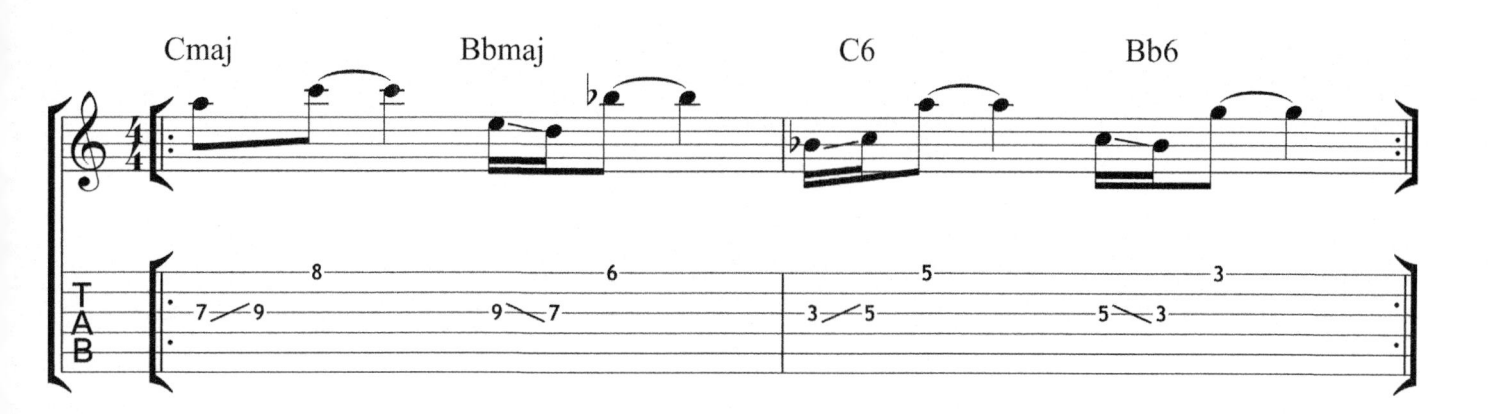

[Musical notation and tablature showing chords: Cmaj, Bbmaj, C6, Bb6]

Hybrid picking comes into its own when playing phrases with notes on non-adjacent strings. Here is a soul-country lick in the style of Steve Cropper. This time, pick the G string downward at the same time as plucking the high E string upward with the second finger. Because the attack of the pick will produce more volume, you can pluck upward a little more aggressively to balance the sound.

Example 1n

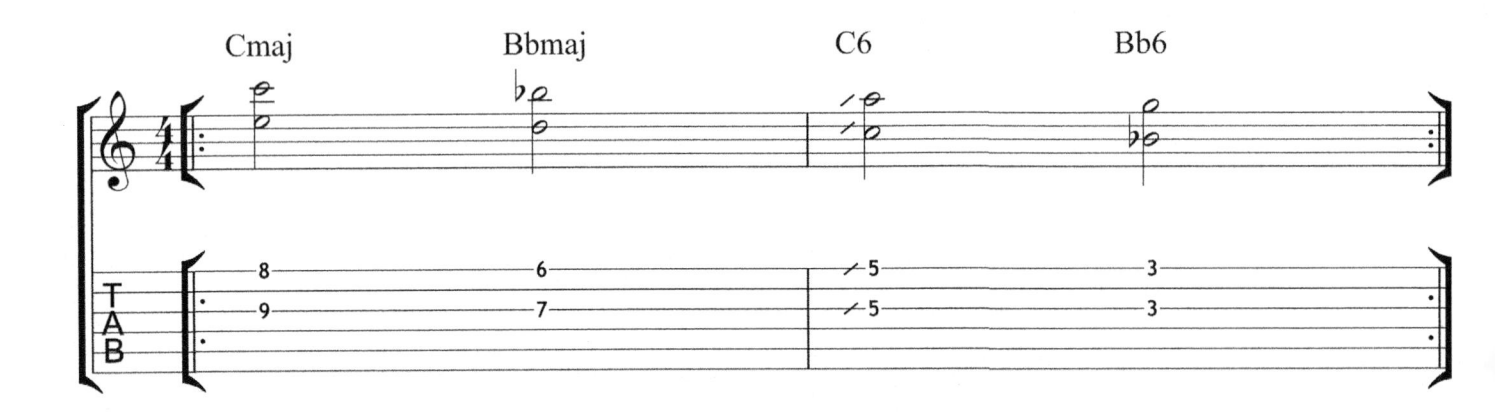

The second type of hybrid picking introduces the third finger into the equation. To play Example 1o using this technique, use the plectrum to downward pick the G string, the second finger to pluck upward on the B string, and the third finger for the high E string.

It's completely normal for this to feel odd and uncomfortable the first time you do it, but with practice it will begin to feel natural. Like fingerpicking, the main challenge is to keep the timing in place and avoid rushing the plucks with the second and third fingers.

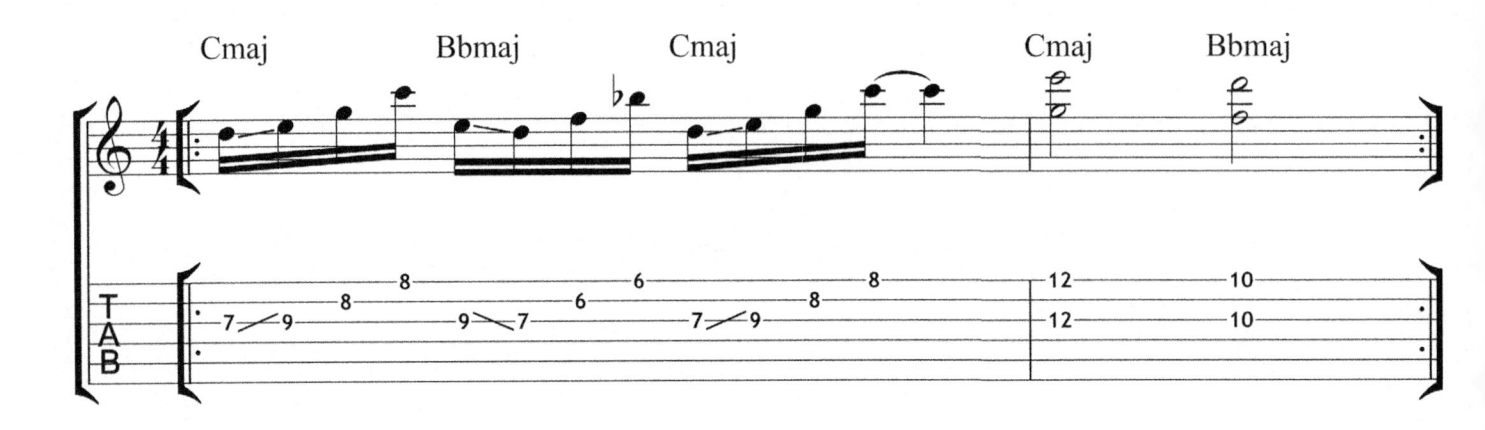

Example 1o

Hybrid picking can be used on any string groupings. In this example, the pick strikes the D string, the second finger plucks the G string, and the third finger plays the B string. In the fretting hand, start with the second finger on the D string and hammer onto the 5th fret with the third finger. This first finger takes care of the notes on the B string.

The shape used in bar one for the G5 is moved down a whole step for the Fsus2 chord.

Example 1p

This next example is designed to emulate a reverse banjo roll.

Playing an idea like this at a slow to medium tempo with just the pick isn't too difficult, but at higher tempos – to really capture that banjo roll effect – hybrid picking makes things much easier. The pick is assigned to the G string, while the second and third fingers take care of the B and high E strings respectively.

Example 1q

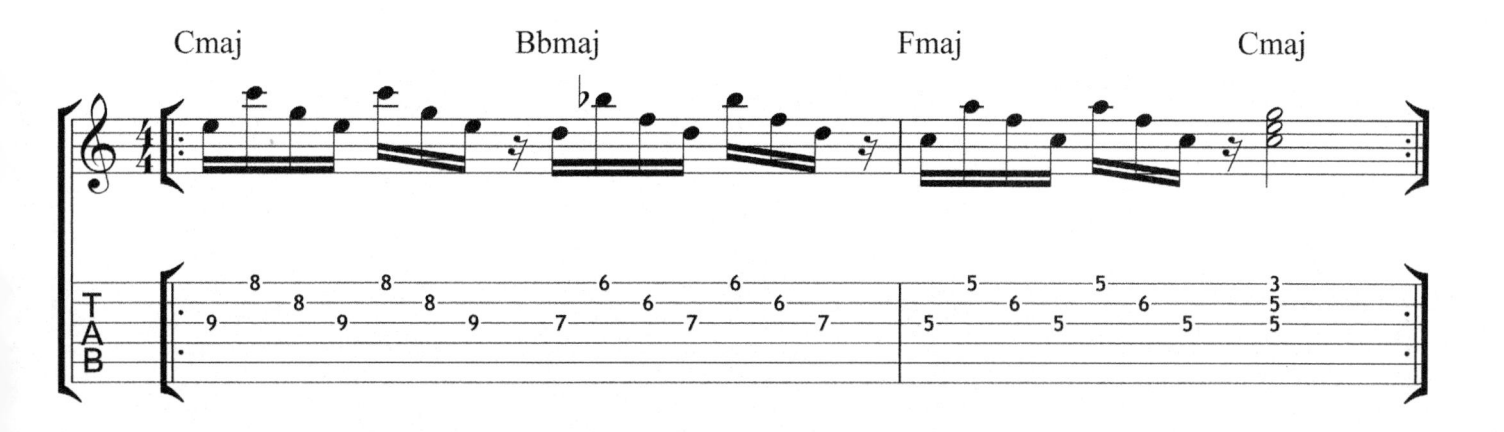

This phrase reverses the previous example to create a banjo lick down the strings. While the notes remain the same and the work the fingers do on the high strings is similar (albeit reversed), you may find this lick easier or harder than the previous example. Personally, I find upward banjo rolls much easier than downward ones.

Example 1r

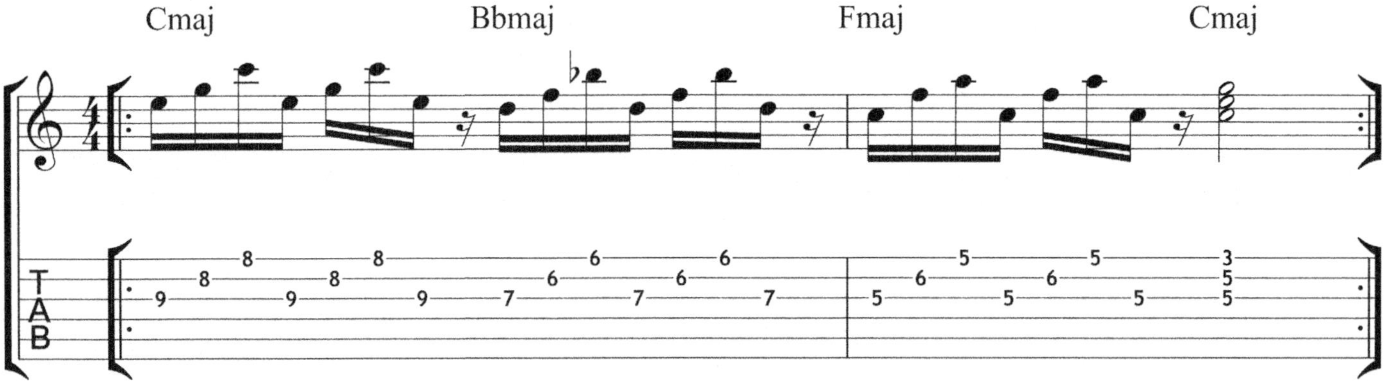
Cmaj
Bbmaj
Fmaj
Cmaj
T
A
B

Remember that one of the great advantages of hybrid picking is being able to pick non-adjacent strings simultaneously. To start this phrase, use the pick on the G string and the third finger on the high E, then pluck the B string with the second finger. This might challenge your coordination to begin with, so learn it slowly and train your fingers to obey!

Example 1s

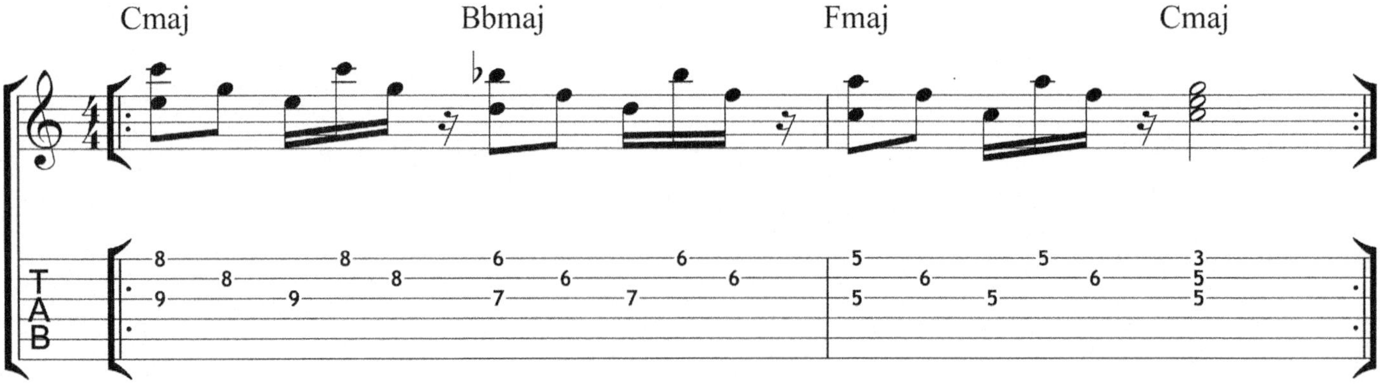
Cmaj
Bbmaj
Fmaj
Cmaj
T
A
B

Here's that example but this time reversed, so we have a downward roll.

Example 1t

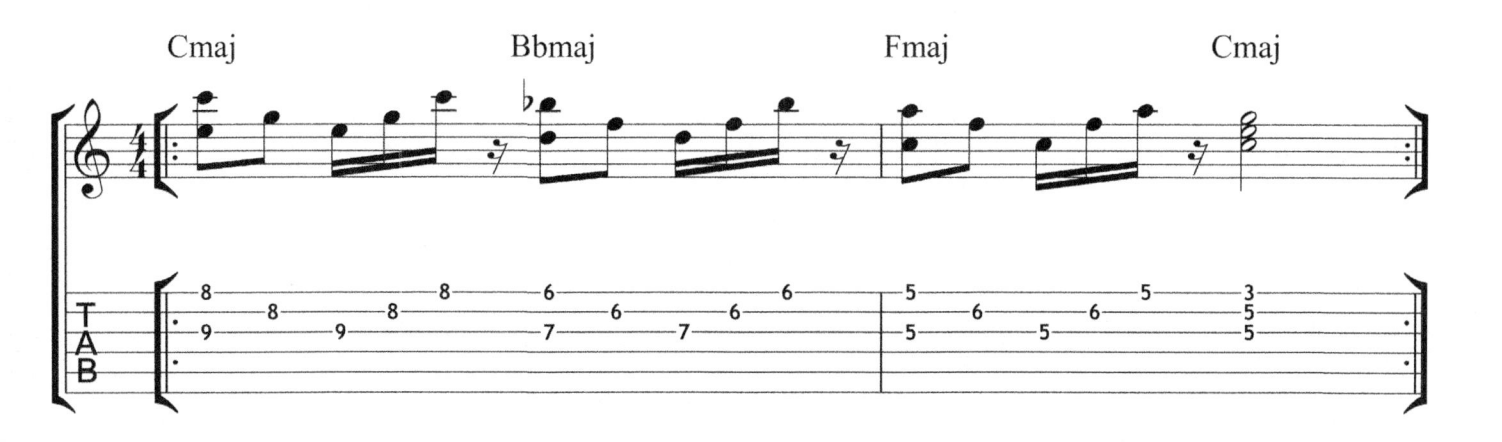

```
       Cmaj                    Bbmaj                   Fmaj                    Cmaj
|------8-------------------8------6-------------------6------5-------------------5------3---|
|---------8-------8------------------6------6-------------------6------6------------5------|
|------9-------------9------------7-------------7---------5-------------5------------5-----|
|------------------------------------------------------------------------------------------|
```

This chapter has been a brief primer on the main picking approaches used in country rock. If you felt equally at home with two or more approaches, this is a great weapon to have in your guitar playing arsenal, and means you can switch picking approaches as the music demands.

If you favoured one approach in particular, which felt natural to you, stick with it for now and focus on refining your technique. But I do recommend exploring all three approaches in your practice times as, ultimately, they will help you to become a more flexible musician.

In the next chapter we move on to look at a staple of country rock guitar technique: string bending.

Chapter Two – An Introduction to String Bending

String bending is one of the most challenging aspects of country rock guitar. While many country rock legends take inspiration from blues guitarists, they also draw from the sounds of the Dobro and pedal steel guitars, which can be emulated via string bending.

To achieve this sound, country rock bends range from standard blues/rock single string bends to double-stop bends, and even "triple-stop" bends that encompass three strings – the closest the guitar can get to sounding like a pedal steel.

This chapter is a string bending primer and will prepare you for the more advanced string bending licks featured in Chapter Three. We will begin with the basic principles of string bending and gradually move on to techniques more focused on the country rock style.

I've said it before, but it's important to be vigilant that you're not playing with any discomfort in the wrist or fingers. Country rock bends (especially triple-stops) can be demanding, so make sure you are warmed up properly and put the guitar down if you get any aches or pains.

Bending with accuracy while injecting emotion is a lifetime's work, so you can never spend too much time practicing bends, even the basic ones. Use the first few examples to warm up and work on bending the notes with a focus on accurate pitching and timing.

To play the bends in Example 2a, use the third finger of the fretting hand and reinforce it by adding the second and first fingers behind it, for extra strength and stability.

Listen to the audio and notice the different note lengths in the notation. These are half-step bends which don't require too much effort, so be careful not to over bend.

Example 2a

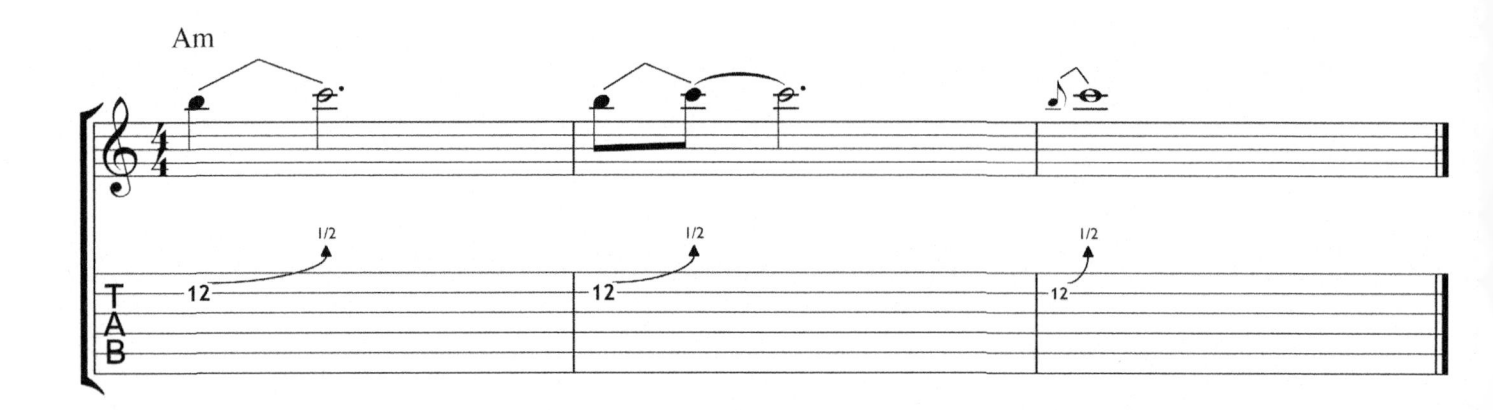

Whole step (two-fret) bends require a greater push from the fretting hand. There is a fine balance to be found between falling short and going too far, so always focus on the pitch – are you sharp or flat? Adhere to the rhythms being played. Part of phrasing a good solo is to be in control of *all* the elements of what we play, and the audio is your guide here.

Example 2b

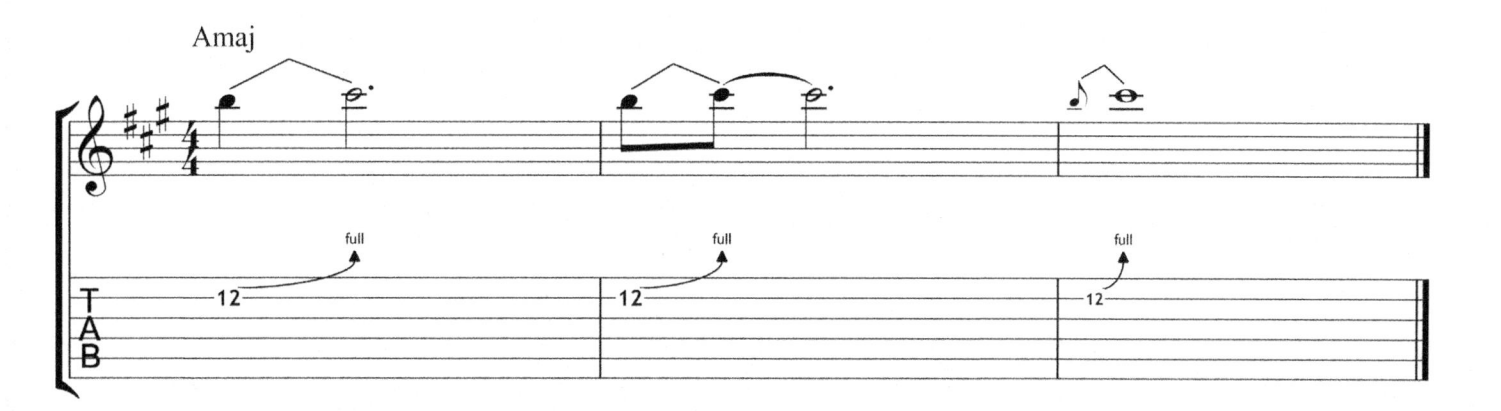

The technique of bending and releasing is a particularly emotive phrasing tool. For this half step bend, use the third finger to bend the note to pitch, keep the pressure on, then release the bend back down to the 12th fret. Gear can cause limits here. A cranked Les Paul through a Marshall will deliver legendary rock sustain, but a single coil pickup guitar through a clean amp won't give you long on the bend.

Example 2c

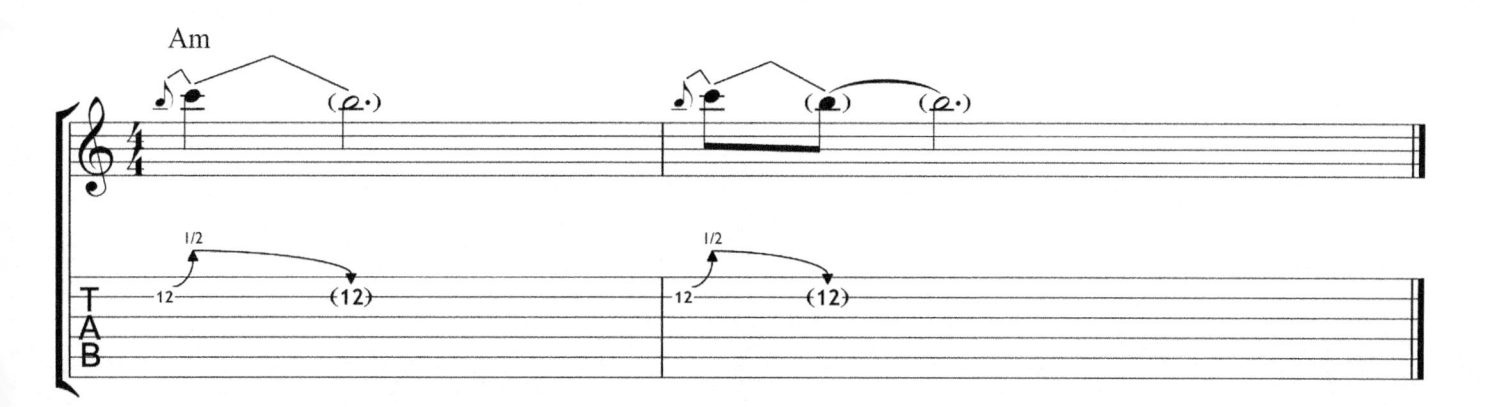

The fingering remains the same for this whole step bend and release. Before moving on, try playing these bends on different strings and frets to gain a better understanding of how string tension affects our ability to bend and demands more or less effort. Bends are easier on the higher frets and harder on the middle to lower frets, where the string tension is greater.

Example 2d

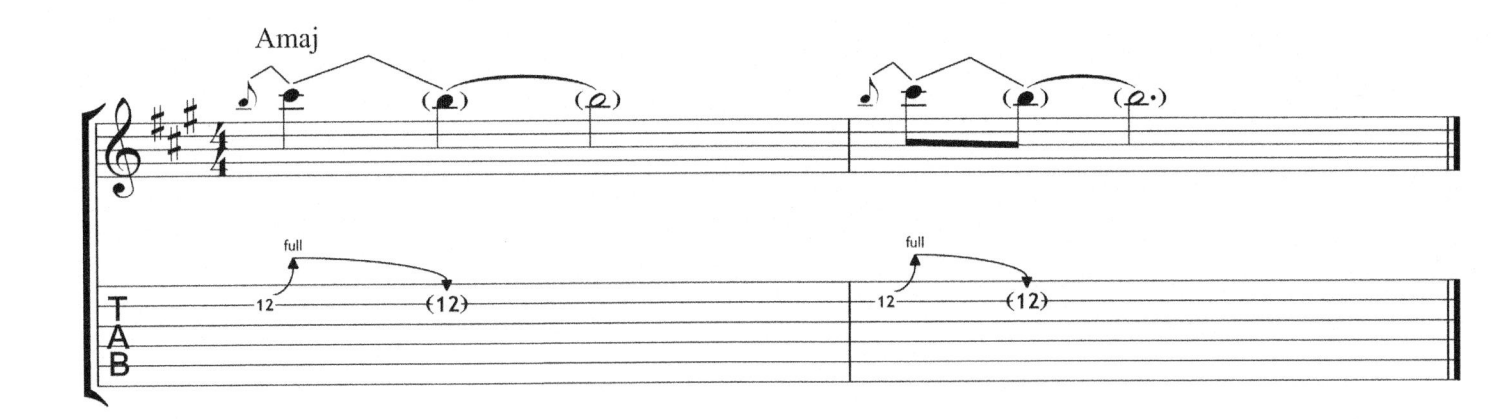

A technique used by many country rock players to emulate the sound of pedal steel and Dobro/slide guitars is the "pre-bend and release". Simply, it means to bend the note before you pick it, then release it after picking. The difficulty is that we have to imagine the location of the bent target note before we hear it, but the previous exercises should help and practicing this is some of the best ear training you can get. Your technique will also improve as you must *feel* where the target note is. Bend the note to pitch with your third finger, then pick the note and release it.

Example 2e

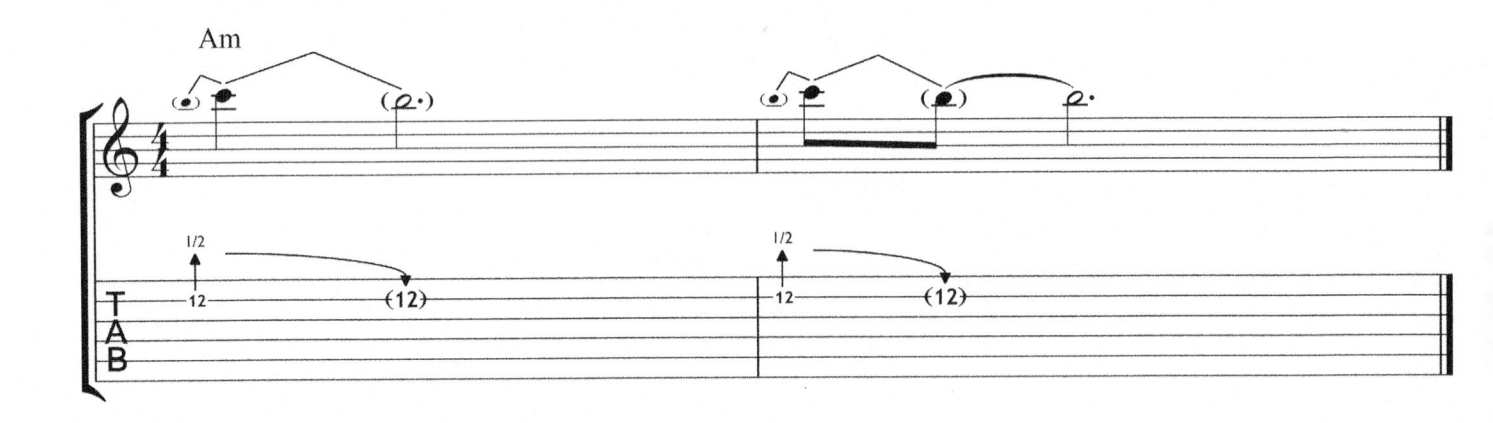

This pre-bend and release exercise takes place over a whole step interval, so initially you will likely find it harder to pitch accurately. But, stick with it, because the end result will be a new, emotive phrasing tool, increased accuracy on the bending finger, and a supercharge to your ear training.

Example 2f

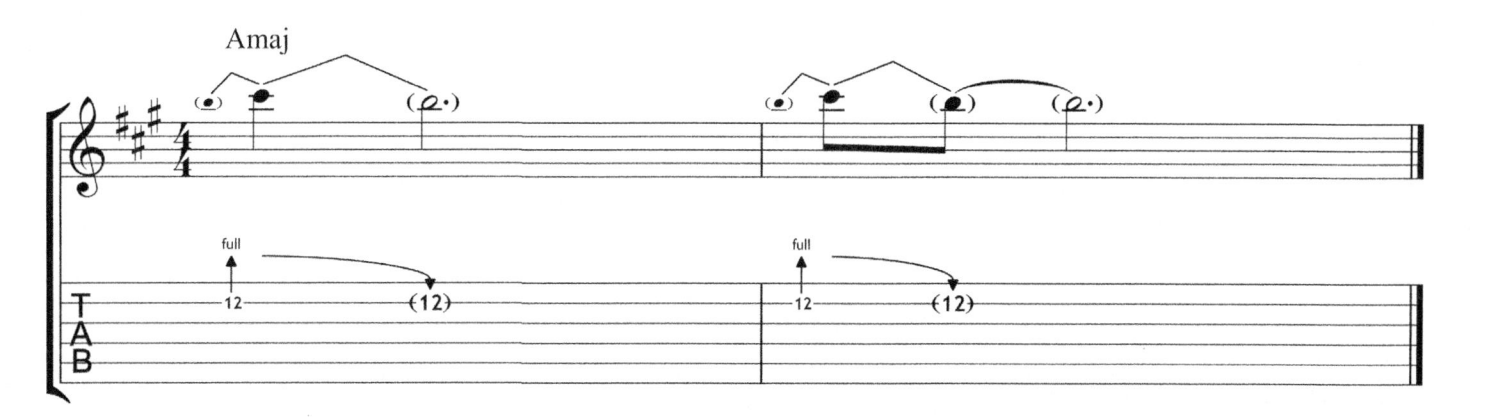

These exercises might appear simple on paper, but don't short-change them, because they are very effective in helping to master pitch accuracy. Now that we've practiced bending single notes, we move on to play bends that include notes on adjacent strings.

In this first example, bend the note on the B string, 12th fret, with the third finger, while simultaneously holding down the high E string, 10th fret with the first finger. The idea is to allow both notes to ring together for maximum pedal steel effect. Over an Am chord, the D note on the high E string makes a cool Am11 sound.

Example 2g

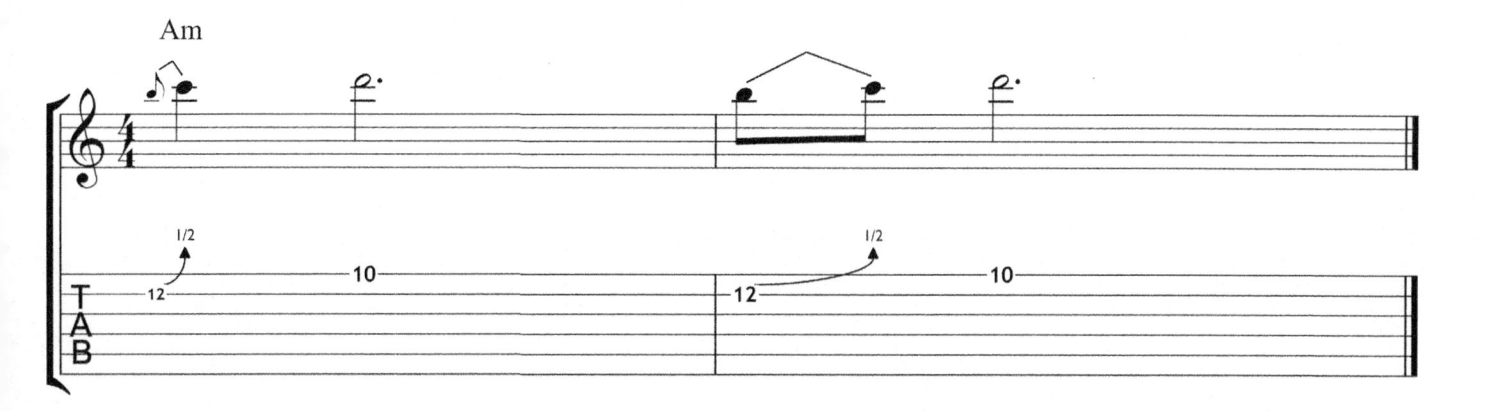

Here is a major sounding bend. This time the third finger bends up a whole step at the 12th fret of the B string, while the fourth finger holds down the note at the 12th fret of the high E string. Allow the notes to ring together as before. Use the first and second fingers behind the third to support the bend. It may feel a little cramped at first, but persevere as you'll use this bend a lot.

Example 2h

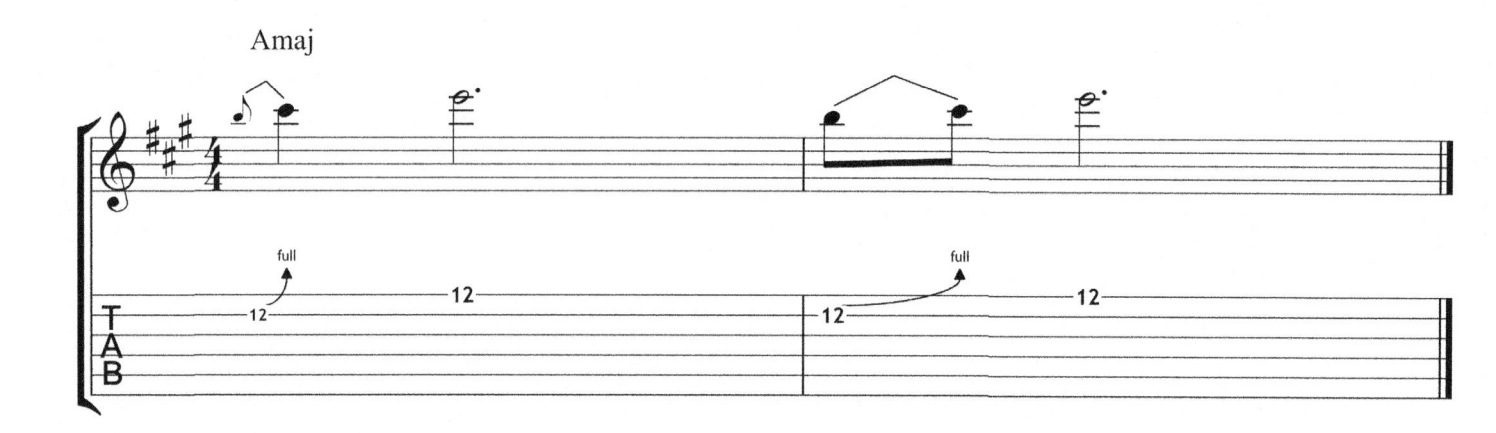

[Musical notation and tablature in A major showing bends at 12th fret]

Next, we're going to play some double-stop bends – two notes bent together at the same time. Double-stop bends really capture the sound of the pedal steel. Here, the third finger will fret the B string, 12th fret, and the first finger the high E, 10th fret. Bend both notes a half step simultaneously. You will hear a clash if the pitch of one or the other note isn't right.

Example 2i

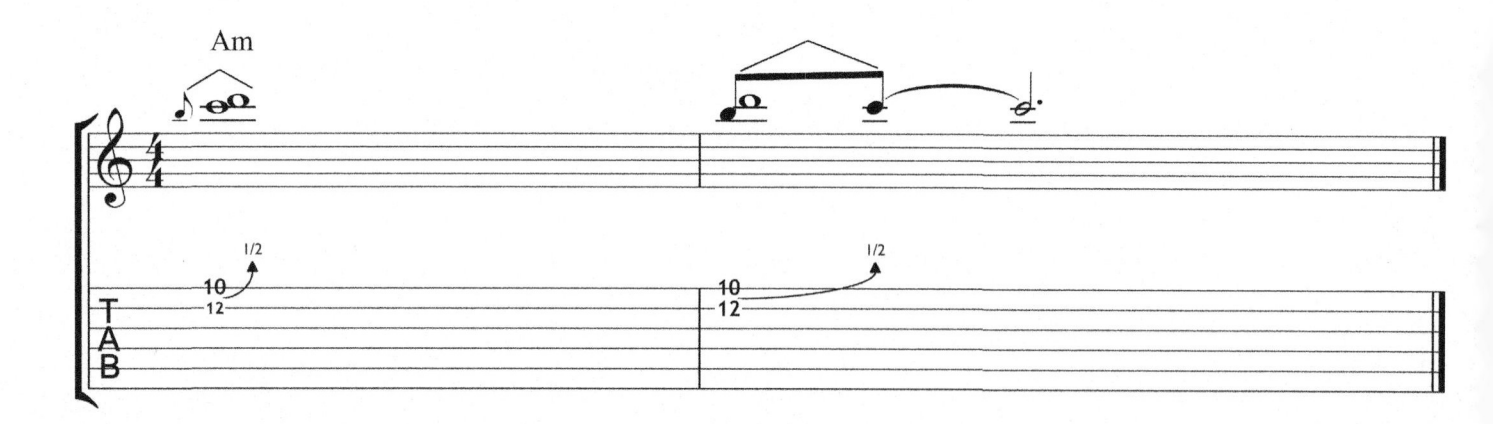

[Musical notation and tablature in Am showing double-stop bends at 10th and 12th frets]

Negotiating double-stop bends can be tricky, as the fingers may feel a little cramped and the angle of the hand may feel awkward. The key to success is a well reinforced bend on the B string and applying enough pressure with the fourth finger at the 12th fret to keep the note in place.

Example 2j

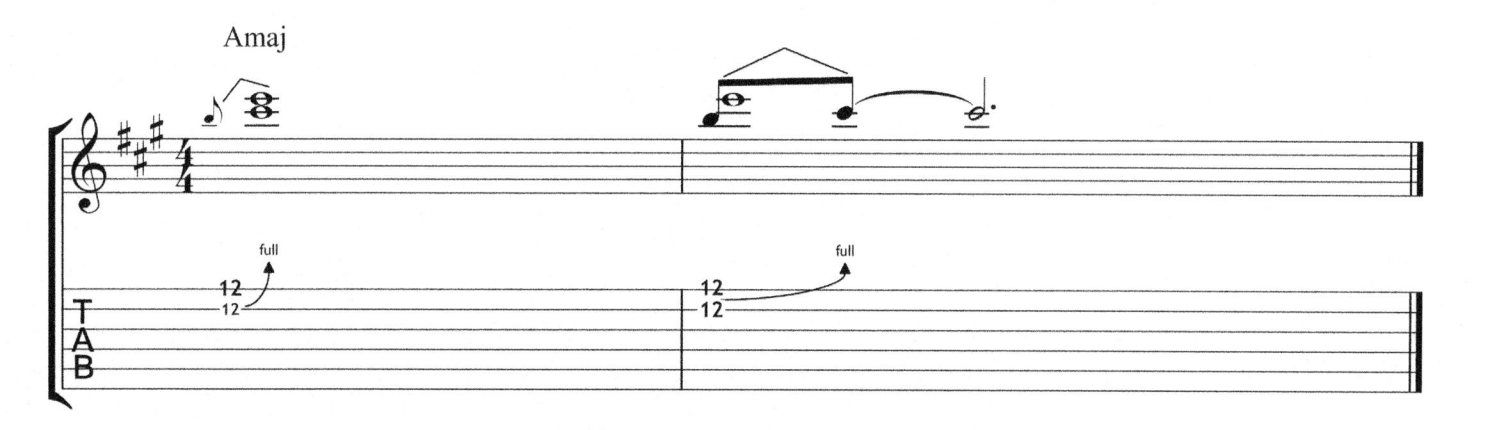

The next example moves the bends over onto the G and B strings. The notes are the same as the previous example, but now arranged on non-adjacent frets. This simple change makes the idea a little easier to play, as the fingers are less bunched up. Use the same finger combination as before in the fretting hand.

In bar one, the notes are bent simultaneously – a double-stop bend – and in bar two they are played separately as before.

Example 2k

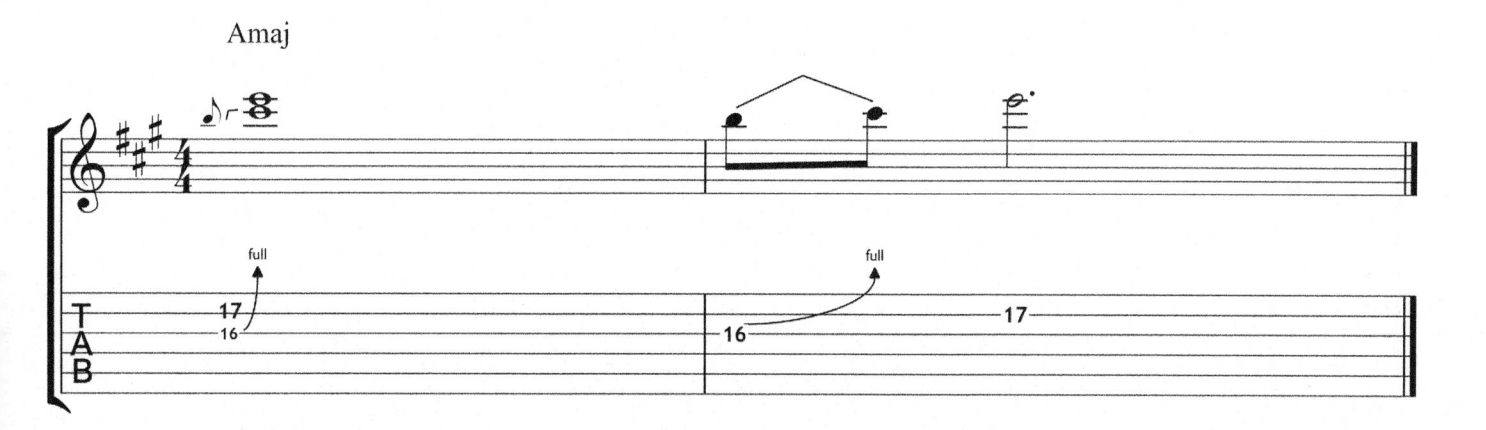

Add more notes and bending exercises start to become licks. In this example, start with a whole-step pre-bend, fretting at the 12th fret using the third finger. Release the bend, then fret the note at the 10th fret with the first finger before returning to the 12th fret for a whole step bend. Try experimenting with the speed of the final bend – it can be quick or drawn out over the remaining beats.

Example 2l

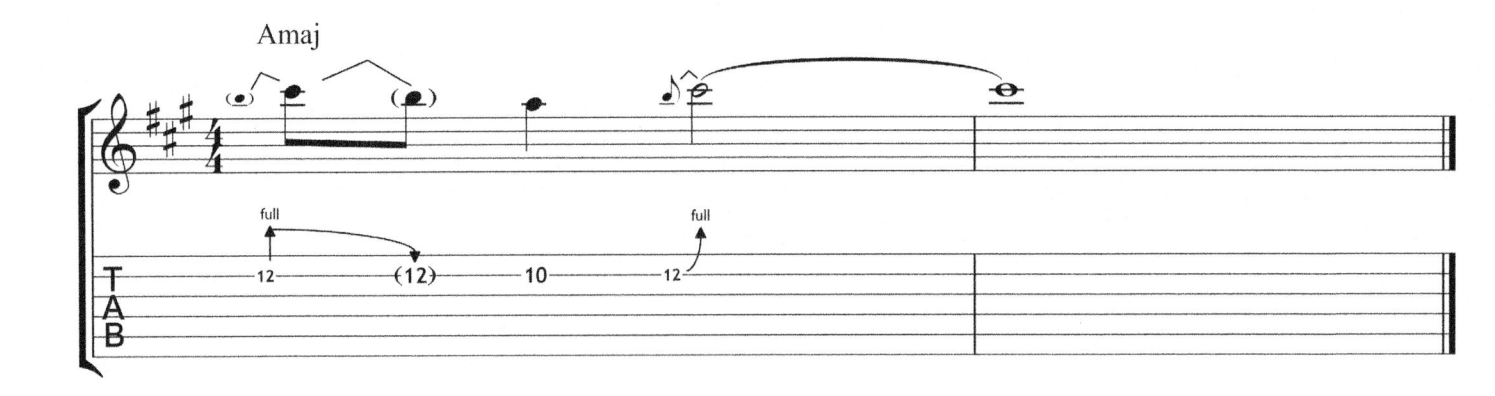

This lick starts with a pedal steel style double-stop bend. You'll recognise it immediately as one of the most well-known country rock licks. Hold down the note on the high E string, 12th fret, throughout and allow it to ring against the other notes. This yields the desired sound and also makes it easier to return to the double-stop at the end of the bar.

Example 2m

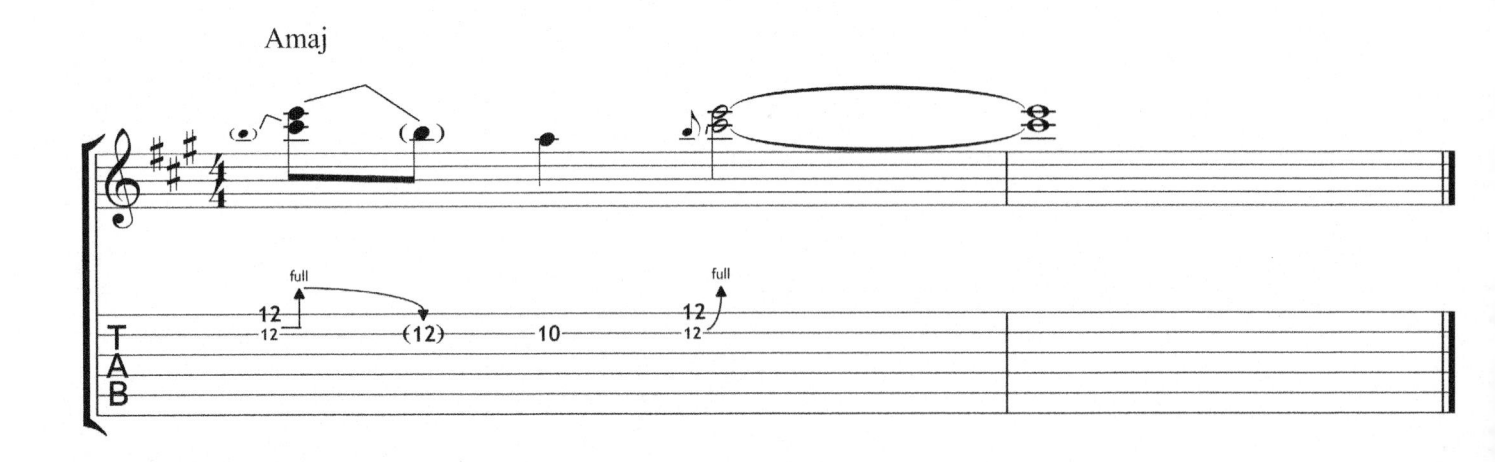

My favourite country rock bend is also one of the most difficult to execute – the legendary triple-stop!

You are picking three strings here and there are several fretting options. Some people use the following approach: the fourth finger on the high E, fret 17; third finger on the B string, fret 17; and the second finger to execute the whole step bend on the G string, with the first finger positioned behind it for extra strength.

The alternative (which is the way I prefer) is to use the fourth finger, partially barred, for both notes at the 17th fret, as this means you can easily use the second finger to take care of the bend, with the first finger behind it for reinforcement.

Strike the strings simultaneously then bend up on the G string.

Example 2n

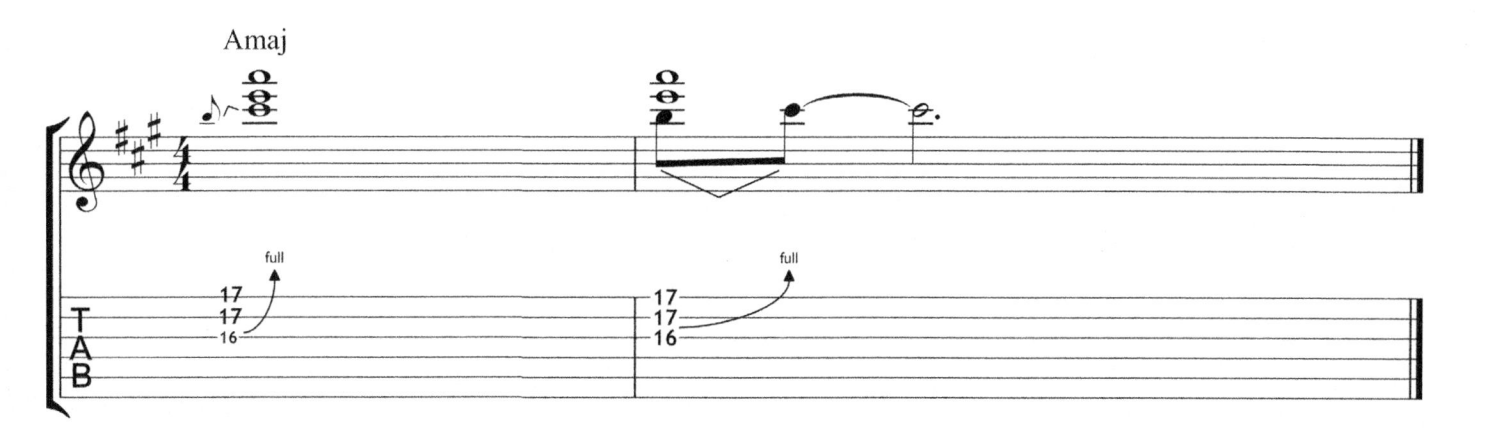

Here's another triple-stop bend. Use the first finger to create a partial barre for the notes on the 5th fret. The second finger will play the half step bend on the G string. This is a pre-bend and release idea, so bend up a half step with the second finger to begin, then pick all the strings together and release the bend.

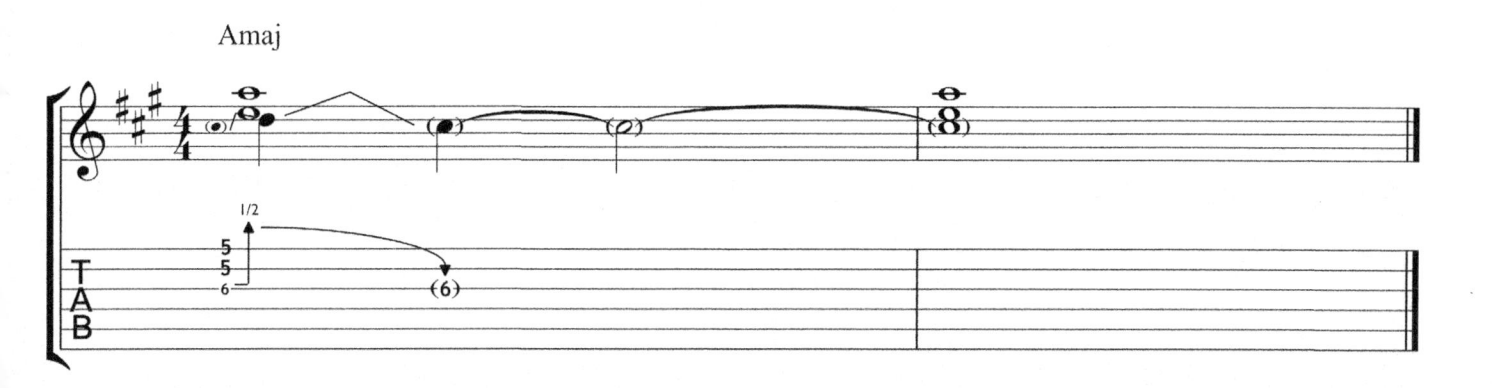

Example 2o

Here's another way to execute the same idea that conjures up the sound of the pedal steel. The fingering remains the same, but the notes are picked consecutively rather than all at once. Prepare the pre-bend before you start, so that you pick the G string then release it.

The most important thing here is to keep holding down the notes after picking them – success is contingent on those notes ringing together!

Example 2p

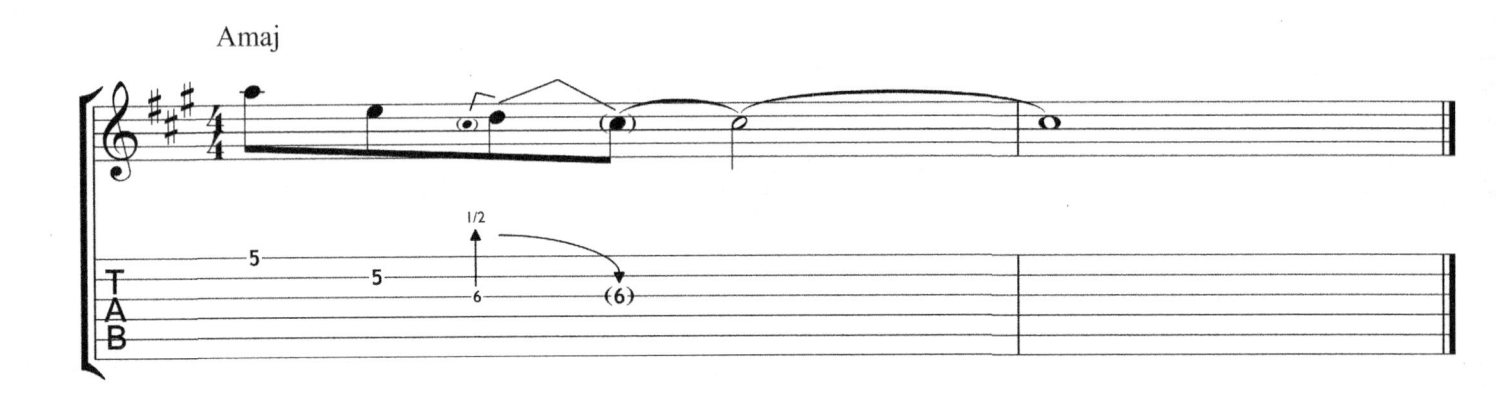

[Musical notation: Amaj chord, tab shows frets 5, 5, 6 with 1/2 bend to (6)]

Let's return to the idea of Example 2n and give it the same treatment, picking the notes consecutively and developing it into more of a lick. Use whichever fingering you preferred from that example.

This time, in bar one there is a pre-bend and release on the G string, 16th fret. Licks like this require some forward planning, as the fingers need to be in place before you pick the first note. The more you play phrases like this, however, the more the fingers will fall into place before they are needed.

Example 2q

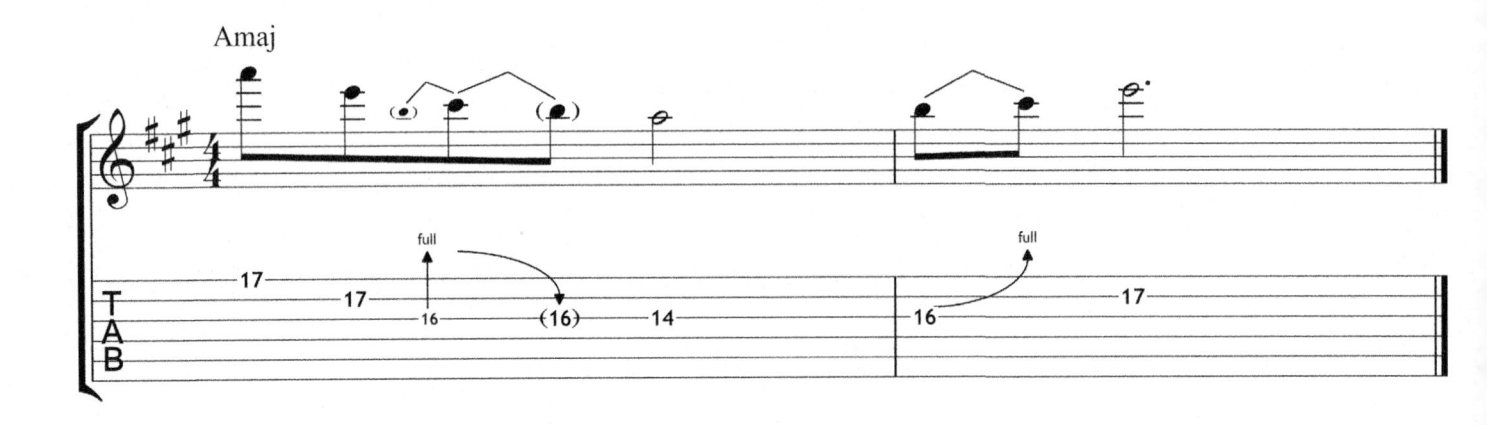

[Musical notation: Amaj chord, tab shows frets 17, 17, 16 with full bend, (16), 14, then 16, 17 with full bend]

This final example will prepare you for the licks to come in Chapter Two. Let's break it down, as we need to think about several things at once here. Use the same fingering from the previous example, and fret all the notes simultaneously.

Pick the G string at the 16th fret, bend up a whole step, then keep the bend in place so that the note continues to sound.

Pick fret 17 on the high E string then return to pick the bent note on the G string.

Now pick the B string, fret 17 before picking the G string and releasing the bend to the 16th fret.

Finally, use the first finger for the 14th fret of the G string.

Take a minute to work through the mechanics of the fingering until you're comfortable with it, then focus on the sound and bending accuracy.

Example 2r

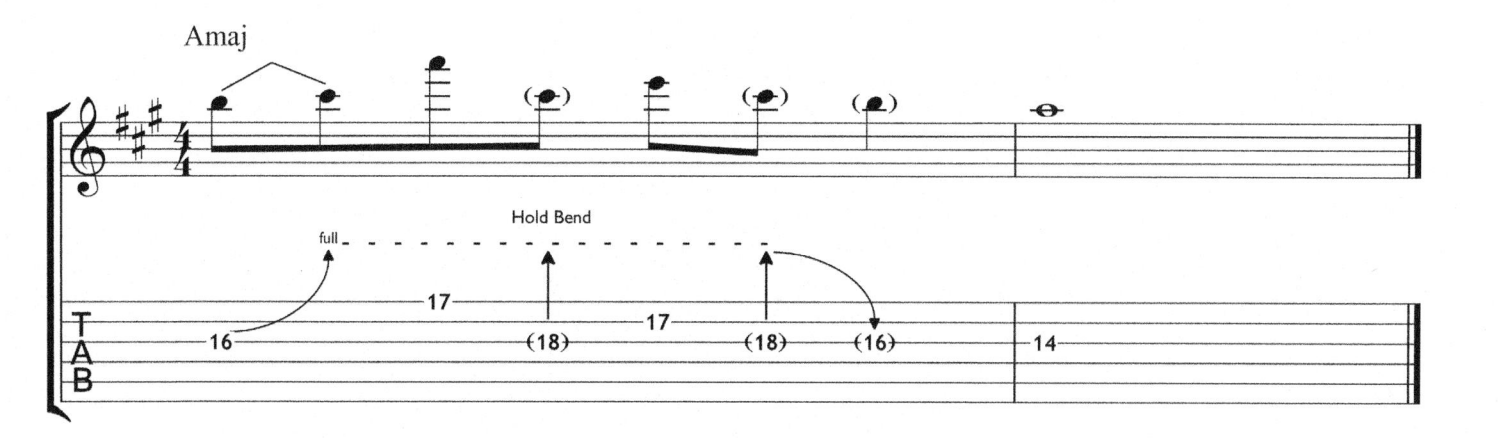

Chapter Three – String Bending Licks

Turning bends into music is where the real fun begins. If you listen widely to country rock music, you'll hear phrases similar to those in this chapter being used time and again. The licks here are based on the string bending techniques you learned in the previous chapter, and move those ideas into the real world, incorporating them into standalone licks. Some of the ideas may appear a little daunting, but think of them as combining various bending techniques you've already studied. If needed, you can always go back and practice one specific element. Tackle each lick by breaking it down into its separate components and follow the performance explanation.

The goal is to work towards playing these ideas comfortably over the backing tracks. Once you've worked out the geography of the lick, playing to the track will help you to focus more on the rhythm and phrasing. It'll also help you to hear if you are pitching the bends accurately. It's easy to bend sharp (too much) or flat (too little), and most players have a tendency towards one way or the other.

With that in mind, let's begin.

Example 3a demonstrates the pedal steel effect over a G major chord groove. Remember that, for a lick like this, you need to plan ahead with your fretting hand finger placement. Before you play a note, place the third finger on the B string, 10th fret, and the fourth finger on the high E, 10th fret.

Bend the B string up a whole step, hold the bend, then pick the E string. Now re-pick the bend before releasing it down to the 10th fret and moving down to the 8th fret.

Example 3a

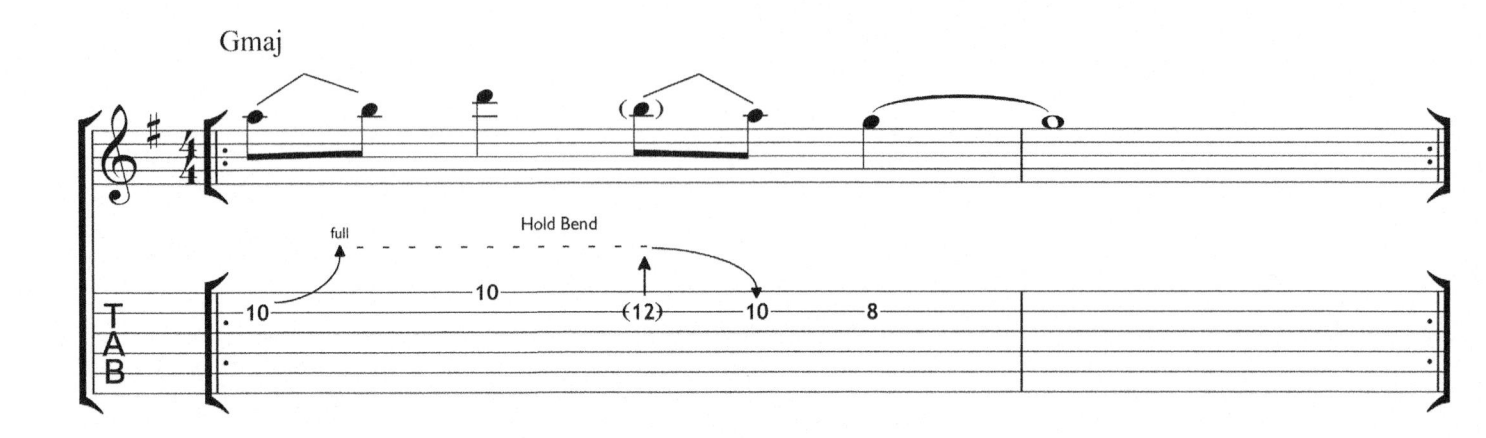

The fingering remains the same for this next example, but here the bend is held, and the high E picked repeatedly before the line moves back to the B string to release it. If you're playing with a light overdrive, as on the audio, the main thing to focus on here is clarity of sound. Pick both strings with the same dynamic/attack so nothing is overshadowed or lost.

Example 3b

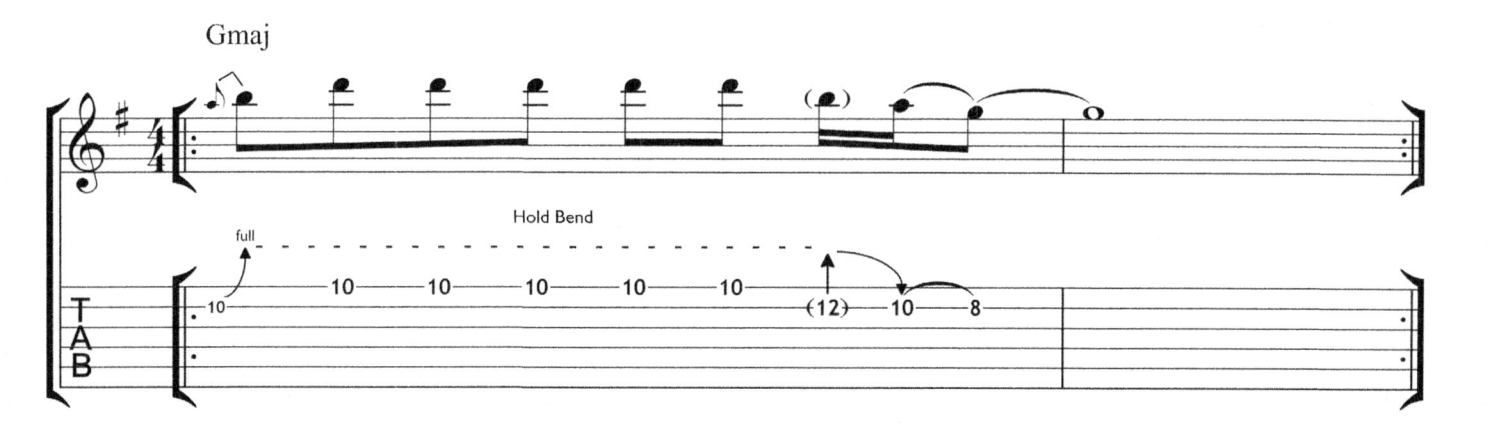

Example 3c is another lick where planning ahead is crucial. Two notes need to be fretted before you begin, so it's almost like playing a chord. Place the first finger on the 8th fret of the high E string and the third finger on the B string, 10th fret. Pre-bend the B string up a tone and now you are ready to start the lick. After the bend is released, the first finger will move over to the 8th fret, B string.

Example 3c

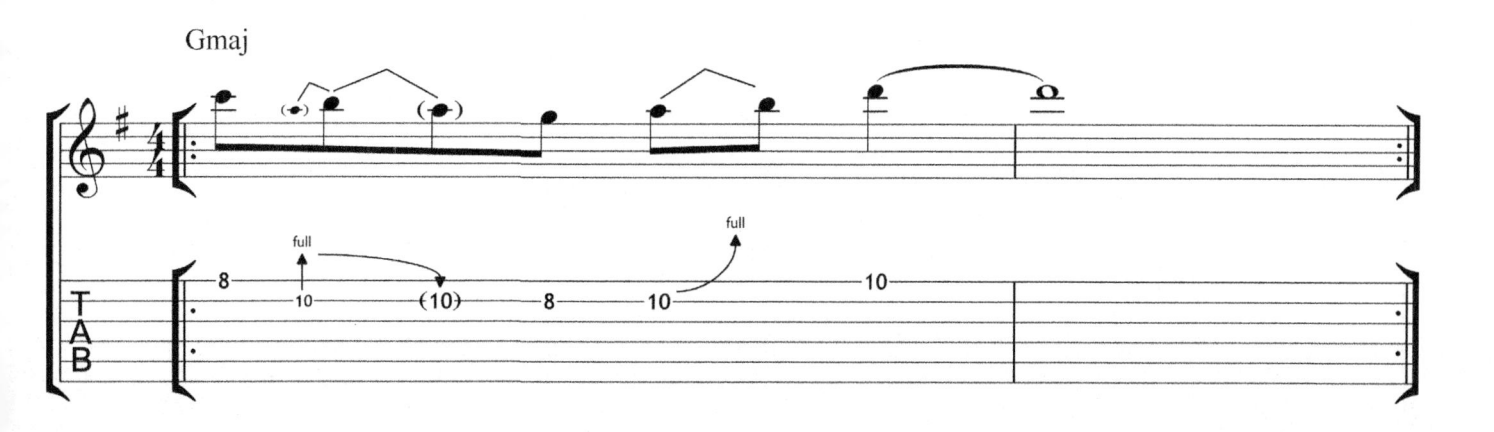

Let's revisit the idea played in Example 3a and develop it further. The challenge here is the movement of the notes on the E string. Use the third finger to play the bend on the B string, 10th fret. Pick and bend it up a whole step, then hold it in place. Use the fourth finger for the E string, 10th fret.

After picking the bent note a second time, move the fourth finger to the 8th fret, still holding the bend. Finally, pick the B string again, release the bend, then slide from the 8th to 6th fret. Play it slowly to begin with to coordinate the fingers and focus on pitch accuracy.

Example 3d

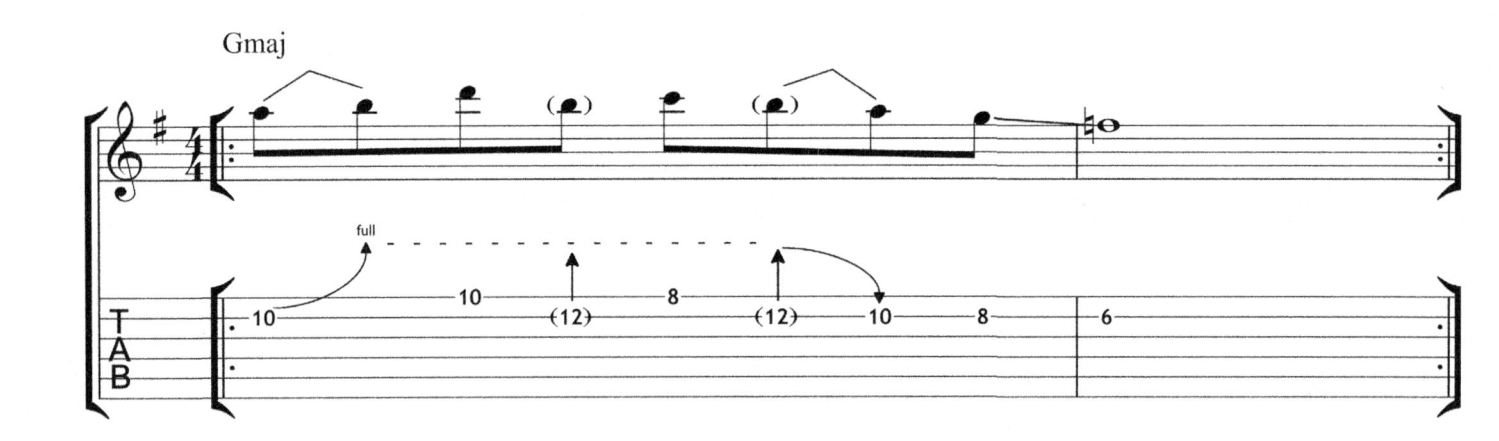

The last lick over this backing track puts the triple-stop bend into practice. Use the fingering option from the previous chapter that felt right for you. The bends within the triple-stop are played rapidly here. After playing bar one, keep the fingers in place until you release the bend on the G string down to the 12th fret with the first finger.

Example 3e

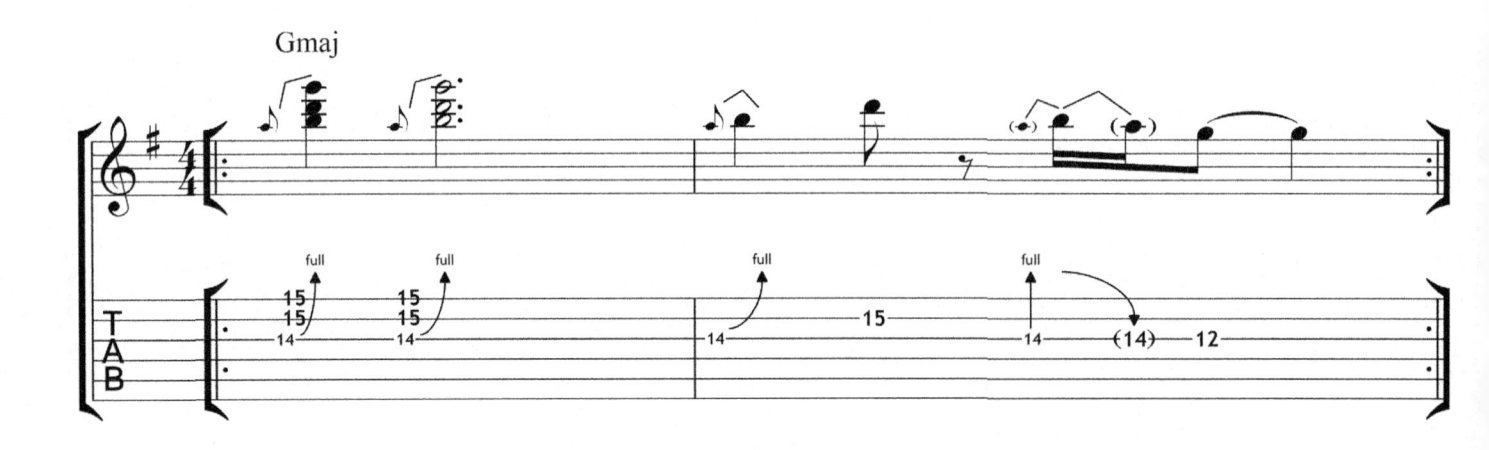

The next track has a different feel and some chord changes to play over. It's a V IV I progression – very common in country rock – played here in D Major (A – G – D). The challenge now is to structure a lick that takes account of the chord changes, and that means aiming for strong chord tones i.e. the root, 3rd or 5th of each chord.

In bar one, use the third finger to bend the B string, 12th fret, while the fourth finger takes care of the 12th fret on the high E. Hold the bend then release it and play the 10th fret.

In bar two, use the first finger on the high E, 10th fret, and the third finger on the B string. You need to prepare the pre-bend on the B string before playing the first note in this bar, so that the notes ring together for the desired pedal steel effect.

Example 3f

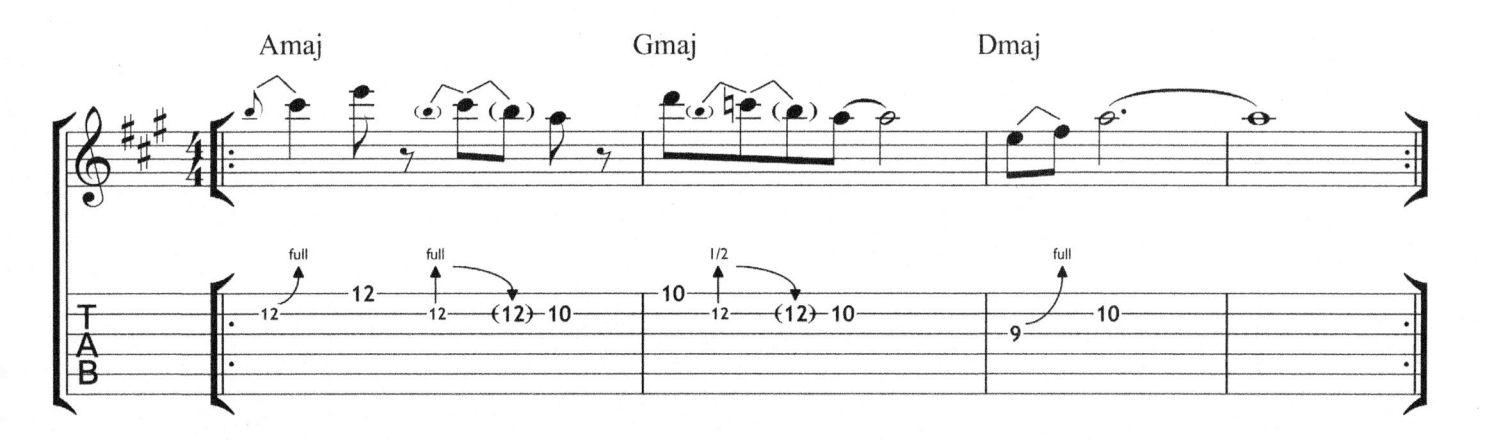

Holding bends and playing them repeatedly is a great sound. Bend a whole step up from the 12th fret on the B string and pick it repeatedly before releasing it. Another cool option is to slowly release the bend while you continue to pick it.

Example 3g

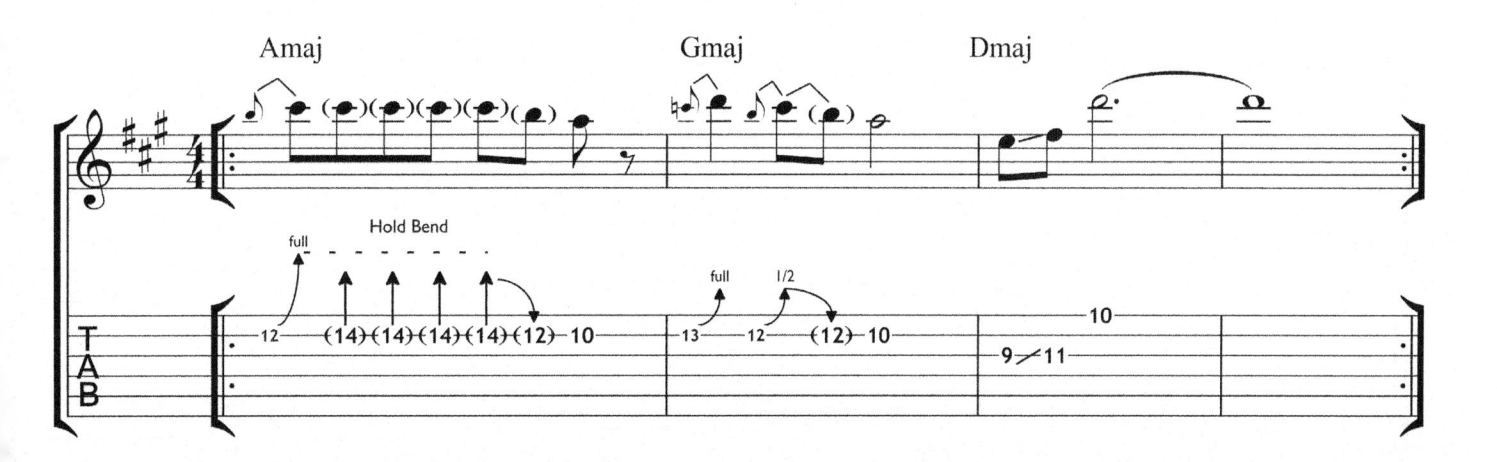

The next lick begins with some more repeat picking on the high E, 17th fret, that simply highlights the root note of the A chord. Playing this note with the third finger is a good option here, as you'll use it for the bend when you move onto the B string. The bend up to an F# note at the 19th fret suggests a Gmaj7 sound over the backing and it is released to a D note, the 5th of the G chord.

In bar three, use the third finger for the G string bend and sustain it while you play the high E, 17th fret with the fourth finger.

Example 3h

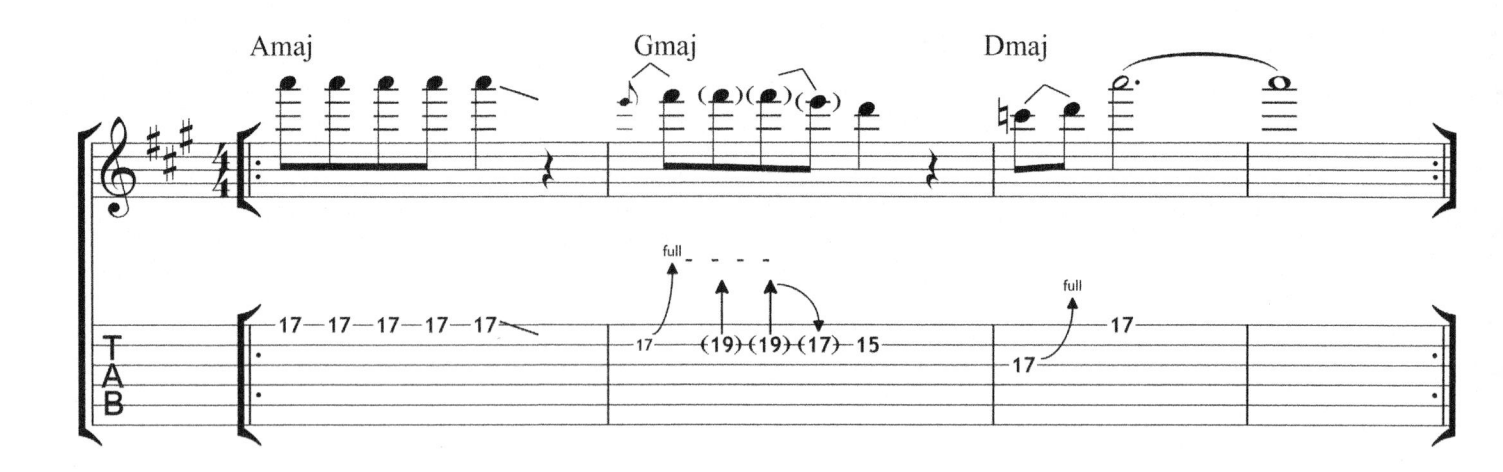

[Musical notation and tablature showing phrases over Amaj, Gmaj, and Dmaj chords]

Combining bluesy phrases with country rock bends will expand your licks even further. This example begins with a blues lick before moving into some bending phrases. Don't overbend the note in bar one – it's a blues curl (a slight pushing of the note, notated here as a quarter bend).

In bar two, execute the B string bend with the third finger (with fingers one and two behind for reinforcement) and fret the high E string notes with the fourth finger.

In bar three, bend with the third finger on the B string again and use the first finger for the note on the high E, 10th fret.

Keep an ear on your pitching. It's a whole step bend in bar two but only a half step bend in bar three.

Example 3i

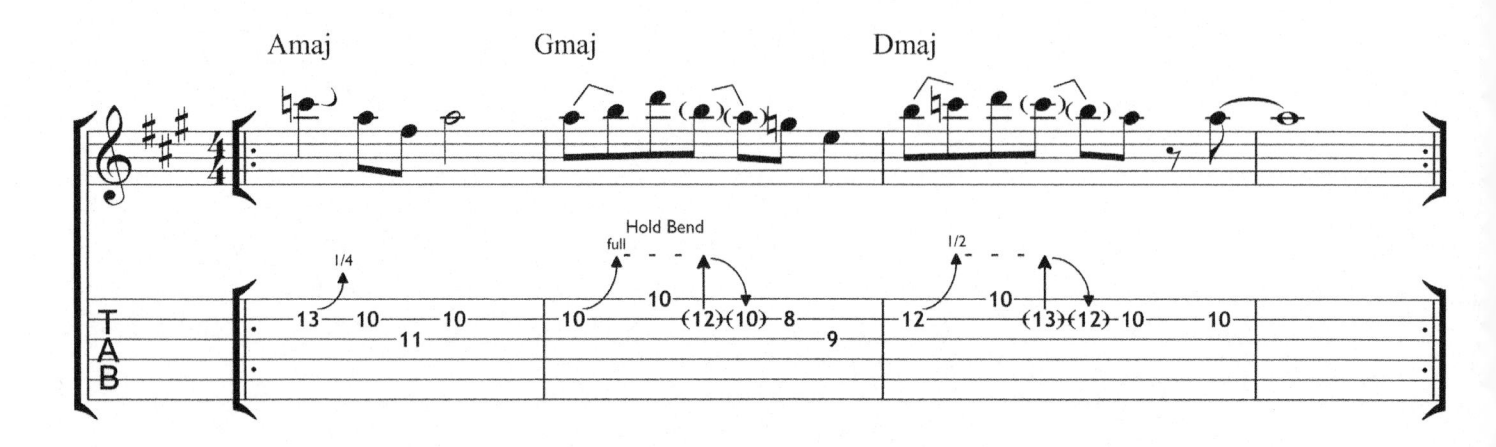

[Musical notation and tablature showing phrases over Amaj, Gmaj, and Dmaj chords]

Transposing a lick to play the same phrase over each chord creates a cohesive idea that the ear can follow. It's also a great shortcut when playing, because the fingering is identical – we just need to shift position. Play this with the third finger executing the bend while the first finger plays the notes on the high E. Due to the higher string tension lower down the neck, you may need to push the bend a little harder for the G chord.

Example 3j

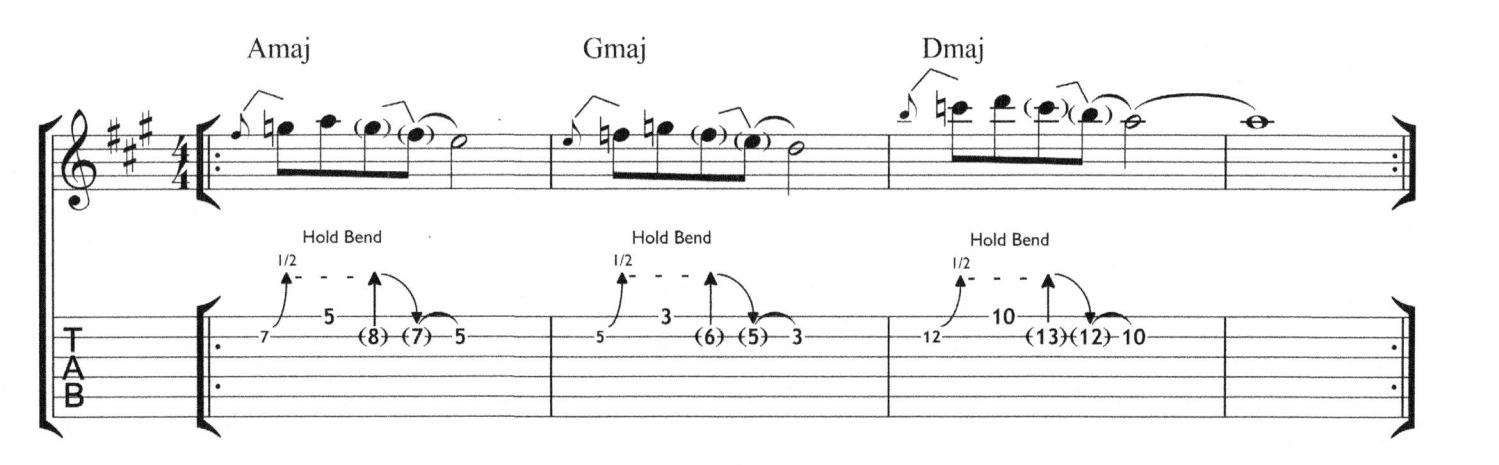

Chapter Four – Harmonised Guitar Parts

A distinctive feature of country rock music is the use of guitars playing in harmony. Think of the outro to *Hotel California* by The Eagles, for example. Take away the harmony part of the guitar solo and you've lost one of the most memorable (and greatest) lead guitar lines in history. The melody to the Allman Brothers' famous tune *Jessica* is another piece that relies heavily on harmonised guitar parts.

In this chapter we'll look at a few similar harmony guitar parts, where we'll break the idea apart and learn each line separately. But also included here are some ideas that can be played by just one guitar. If we want to fatten out a guitar line, playing two-note structures is a great approach. Think of the melody played in 3rds that provides the main hook for Van Morrison's *Brown Eyed Girl*, for instance – a great use of a harmonised line played by one guitarist.

The most common intervals used for harmonies in country rock are 3rds, 5ths and 6ths, so these will be the focus of this chapter.

You probably already have an understanding of how harmonised guitar parts work, but for completeness let's spell it out simply.

Here is the G Major scale, harmonised in 3rds. Bar one shows the scale played from the root note, while bar two mirrors the scale with each note sounding a 3rd above (i.e., the first note of bar one is G, while the first note of bar two is B – an interval of a 3rd).

There are three audio files relating to Example 4a, so that you can hear each part played separately, and both played together. Play the harmony line along to the example played from the root note, and vice versa.

Example 4a

Example 4b takes the harmonised notes of the previous example and plays them together as one part. It immediately creates a fat sounding part, and you can imagine using parts of this idea to flesh out a rhythm part.

Notice that the idea has been extended into the next octave. Also notice that the fingering has altered from the previous example. I've arranged the fingering in a logical manner, to make the idea easier to play in harmony, but there are other ways to finger it and you can experiment.

Example 4b

Let’s repeat this exercise, but this time using 5th intervals. Here is the G Major scale harmonised in 5ths. You’ll hear that this interval gives a thick, solid sound. It’s good for riffs low down on the neck, but also for higher parts to thicken out a melody.

Example 4c

Here is the same thing played by one guitar. You’ll recognise this interval’s “power chord” sound throughout this exercise.

Example 4d

Lines arranged in intervals of a 6th lie at the heart of the country guitar sound, so it's well worth spending time practicing this sound. Here is the G Major scale arranged in 6ths.

Example 4e

Due to the wider interval distance from the root note, 6ths are usually arranged on non-adjacent strings. Because of their layout on the fretboard, hybrid picking works well to play them, otherwise some awkward string muting is required. Try the hybrid approach by picking the lower notes with the plectrum and using the second finger to pluck the higher note.

Example 4f

Now that we've looked at the main ways of harmonising a scale and playing it, it's time to apply these ideas in some licks. Harmonies come alive in context and this means applying rhythm and melody.

This Allman Brothers-inspired phrase is written in thirds. Good timing is critical when playing harmony lines. If we push ahead or lag behind the other guitar part, it will result in a swirling effect known as *phasing*. Practice both parts over the appropriate backing and, if you can, record yourself playing the lines so you can test your timing.

Example 4g

For a different effect, in Example 4h, guitar one from the previous example is harmonised in 5ths, but only in the first bar. When creating harmony parts, both instruments don't have to stick strictly to the same harmonic interval, or even move in the same direction. At the start of bar two, guitar two moves down while guitar one moves up.

Example 4h

Next, here is the sound of 6ths in the context of a lick – again played against guitar one from Example 4g.

Example 4i

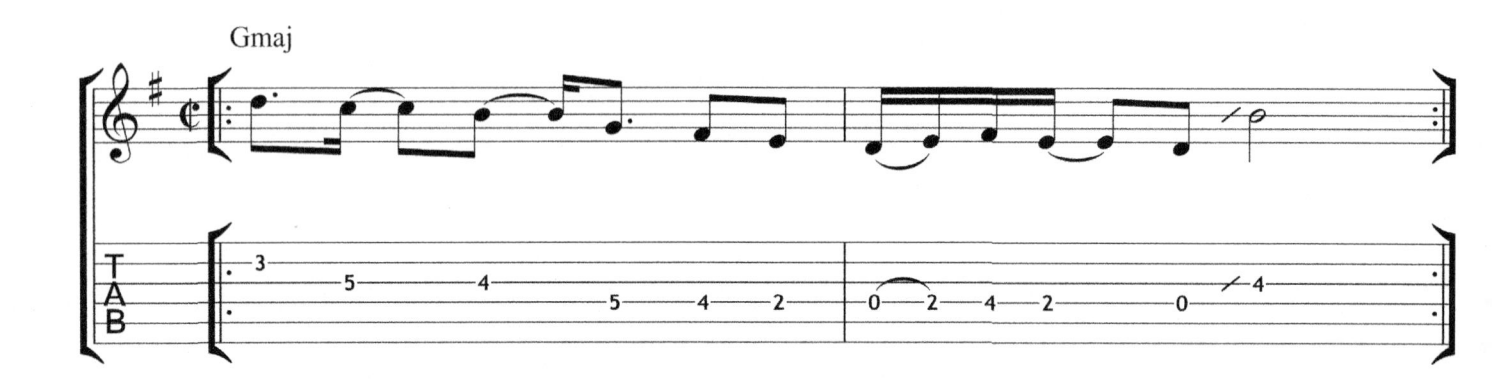

[Musical notation in Gmaj with tablature:
3-5-4-5-4-2-0-2-4-2-0-4]

This example combines intervals, played over guitar one from Example 4g. Notice that mixing up the intervals produces a quite different sound. Remember, you don't need to stick rigidly to one harmonic interval. Notice that this example is played in the octave below guitar one and in bar one moves up while the original part moves down.

Example 4j

[Musical notation in Gmaj with tablature:
5-7-5-7-9-7-9-7-9-7-8-12]

Another Allman Brothers-inspired lick highlights a slightly different way to use guitar harmony. Here, we are harmonising a bluesy C Minor Pentatonic scale lick, using the easiest of all harmonies – an octave. Guitar two doubles up the line played by guitar one an octave below. While octaves don't result in the sweet sound of 3rds or 6ths, they have a really cool fattening effect.

Example 4k

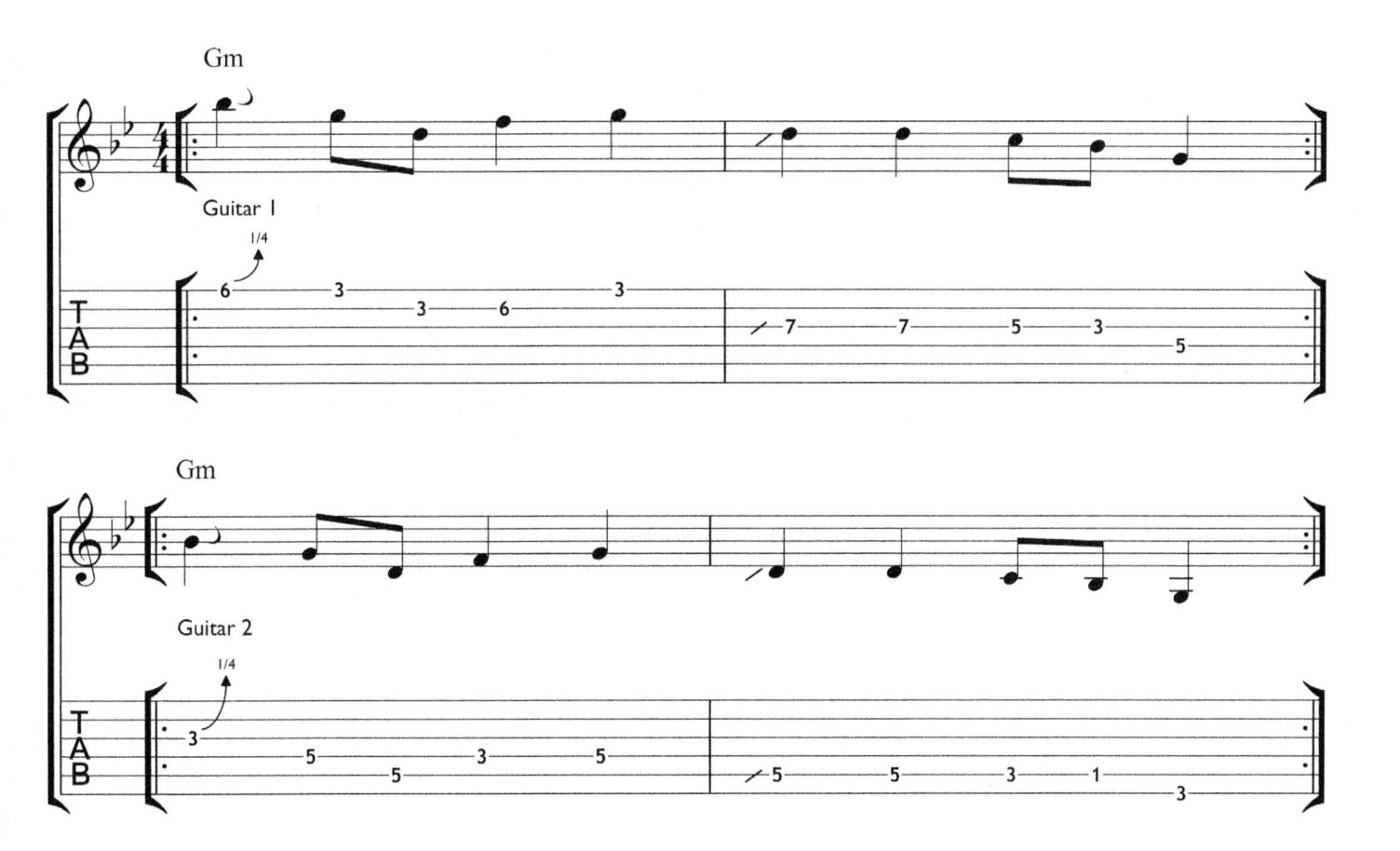

[Musical notation and guitar tablature for two guitars in Gm]

The Eagles used the minor pentatonic scale to write classic riffs like *Life in the Fast Line*. This example builds a riff using the E Minor Pentatonic scale, which guitar two harmonises an octave higher. The key to success with parts like this is to use cohesive rhythms and a strong sense of melody.

Example 41

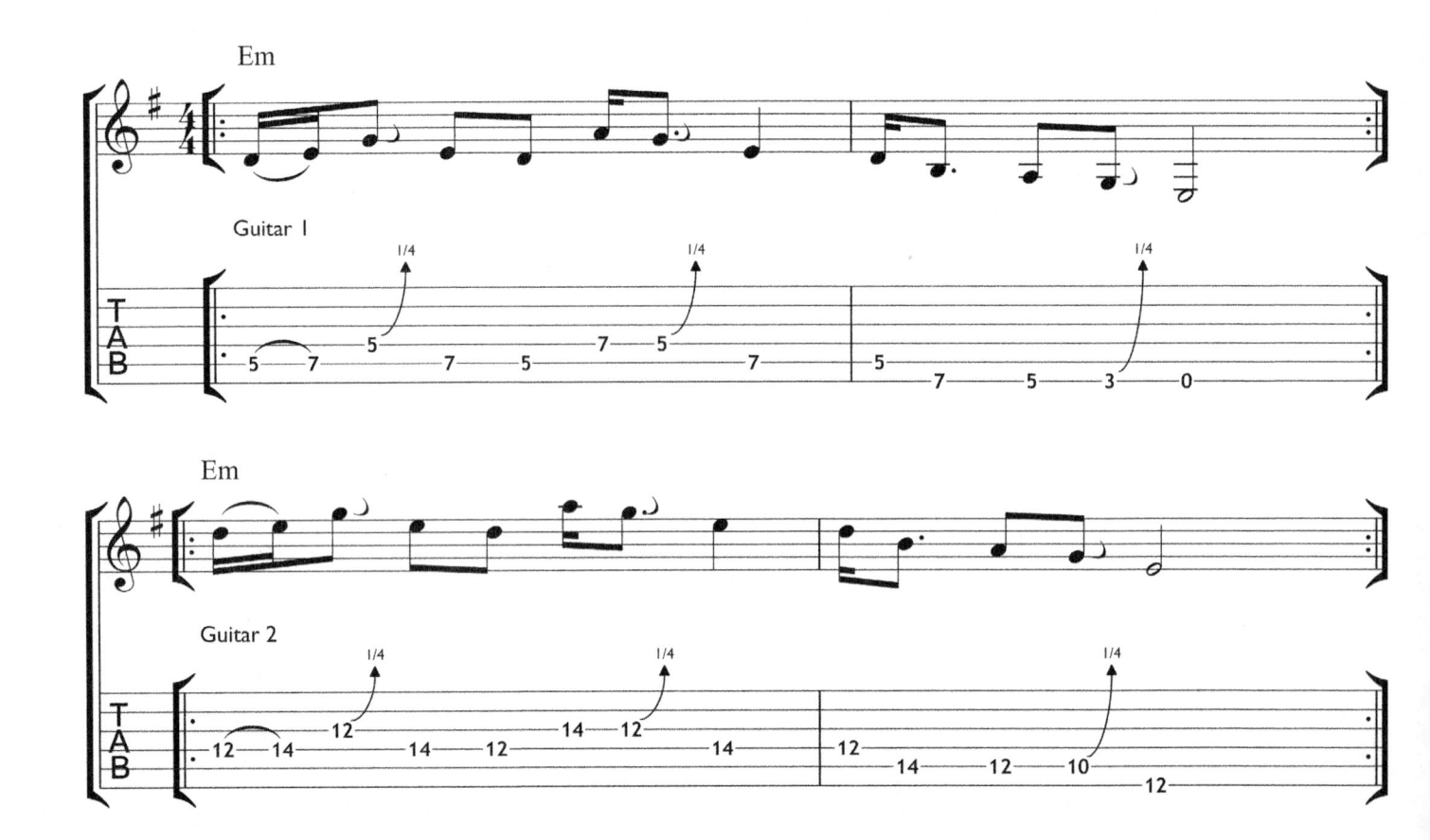

Sticking with the minor pentatonic scale, here's another lick in the style of the Allman Brothers that uses C Minor Pentatonic arranged in 5ths. The triplet rhythm makes this more challenging as you have to fit three notes into the space of each beat, but you can play both guitar parts using just the first and third fingers of the fretting hand.

Example 4m

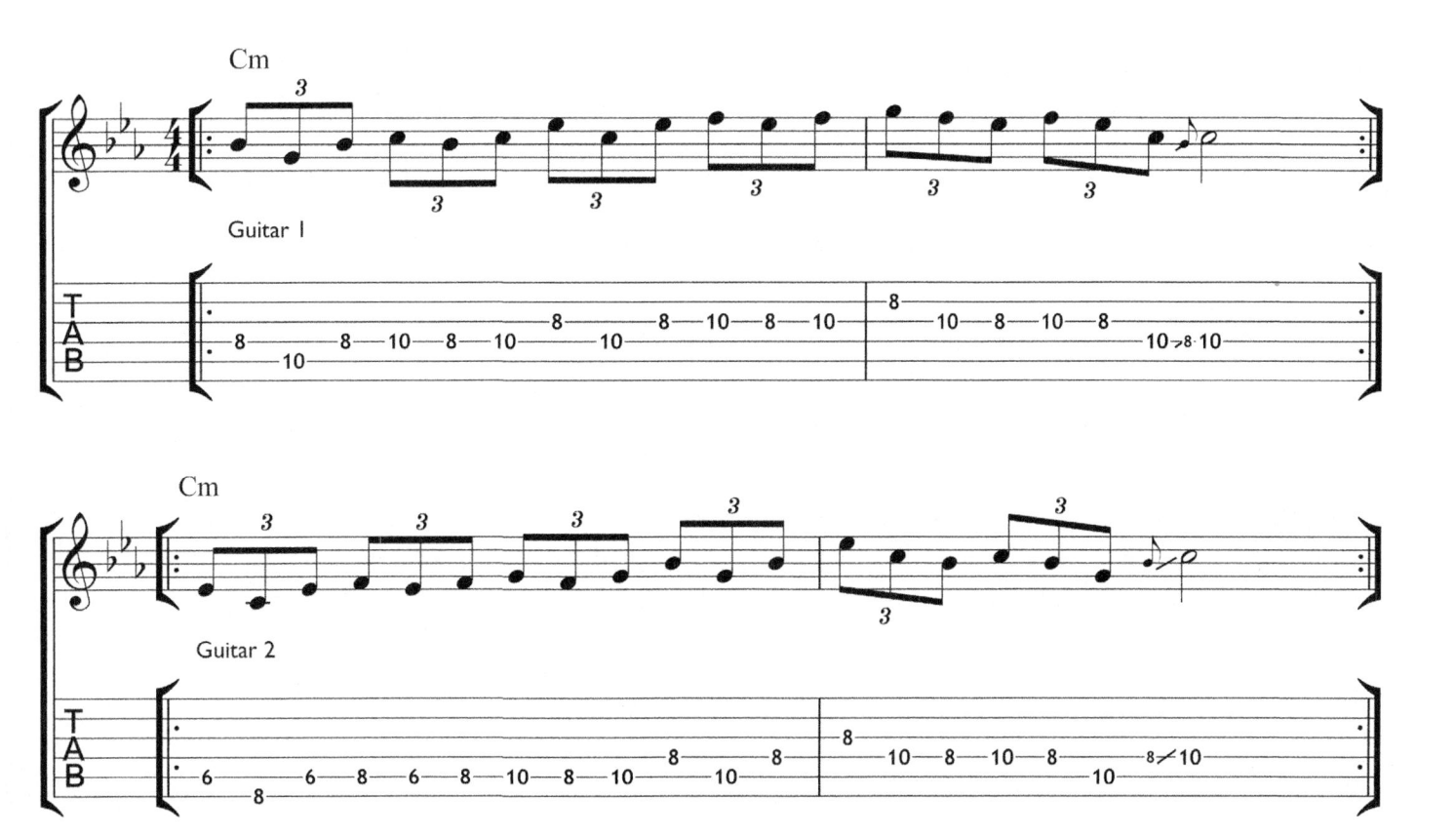

The outro from *Hotel California* is rightfully one of the most famous harmony parts of all time. While it sounds complex, it's actually based on a very simple approach to harmony – layering arpeggios on top of each other. In this example, both guitars play variations of the same three-note arpeggios to yield a fantastic, full sound.

Example 4n

Here is another Eagles-inspired lick that uses the G Major scale and harmonies built on 3rds. Bar two uses some of the country bending lick ideas you studied earlier to create a cool, harmonised pedal steel effect. Strive for accuracy in your pitching here, because the potential for phasing is greater when bending notes.

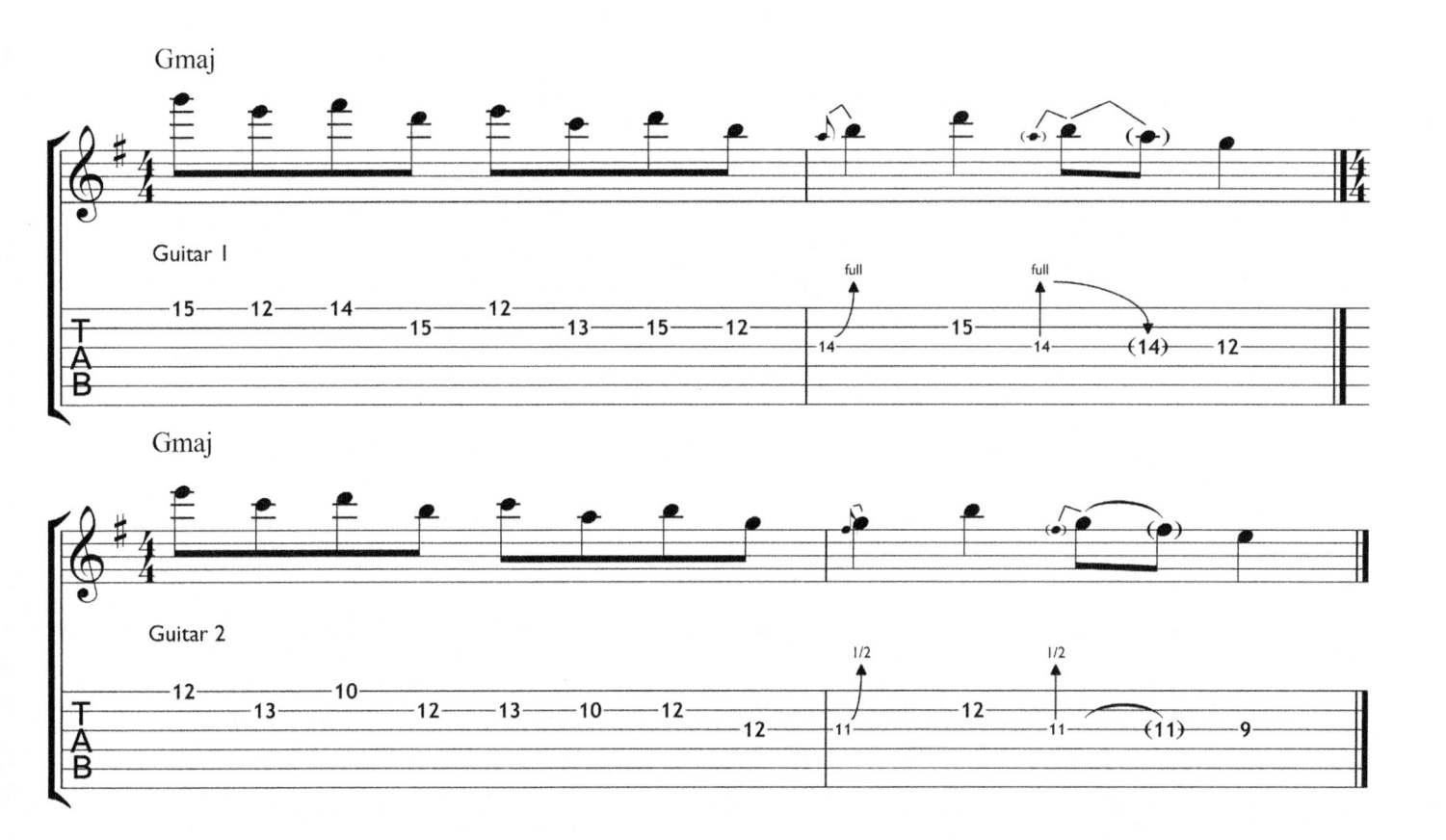

Example 4o

Gmaj

Guitar 1

```
-15----12----14-------12---------------------------full----------full---------
-----------15-------------13----15----12---14------15-------14---(14)---12----
```

Gmaj

Guitar 2

```
-12-------10---------------------------1/2--------1/2---------
---13-------12---13---10---12----12----11----12---11----(11)---9---
```

This time, guitar two harmonises the lick in 5ths. Phrases in 5ths work well higher up the neck, as the higher pitch brings more clarity. Reserve 5ths low down the neck for chunky riffs!

Example 4p

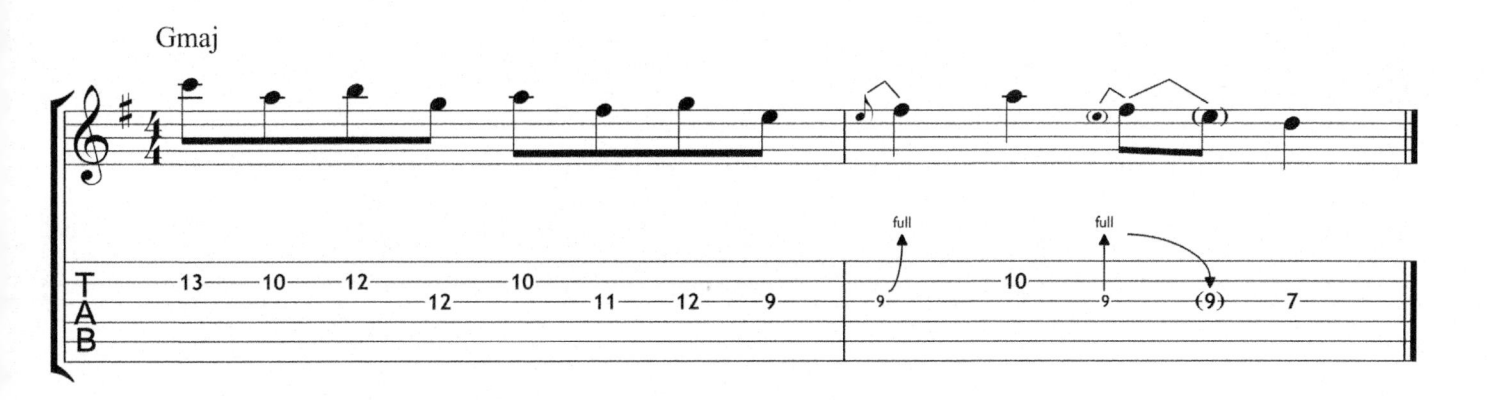

Gmaj

```
-13---10---12-------10--------------------full------full-------
---------12----11----12---9---9------10----9----(9)---7--
```

43

Finally, the original lick is harmonised in 6ths. This one requires a bit of finger dexterity, so begin with the fourth finger on the B string, and the third finger on the G string. Then fret the note on the B string, 10th fret with the first finger, while the second finger takes care of the G string, 11th fret, followed by the third finger at the 12th. The first finger will now drop back to play the G string, 9th fret. The third/fourth fingers will take care of the notes on frets 11/12 respectively to complete the bar.

Example 4q

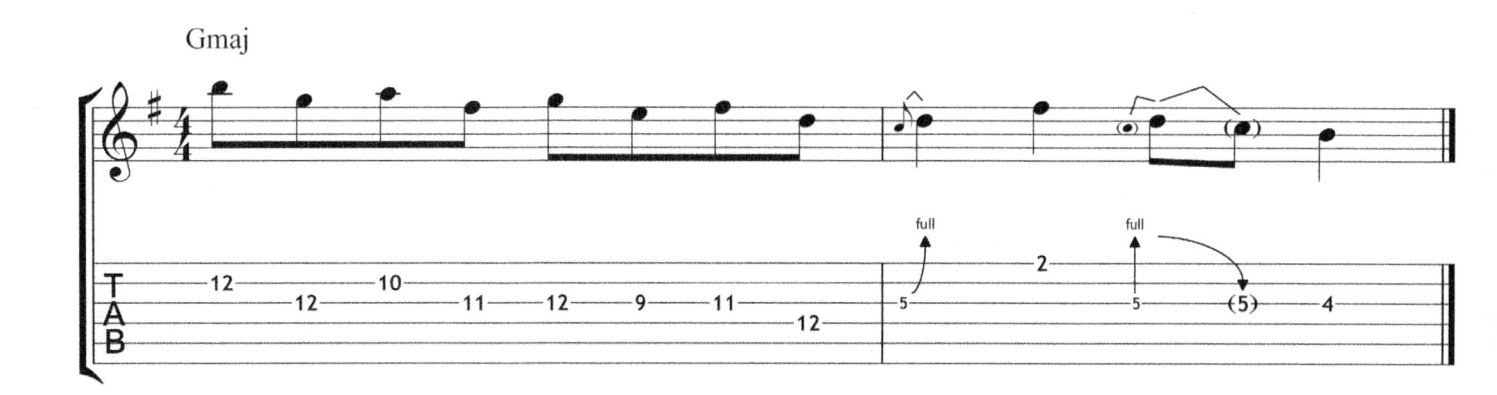

Intervals of 4ths, which we've not explored until now, are typically used to create double-stops in country rock. 4ths are another useful device for fattening up licks, but also serve as a great riff-writing tool. Perhaps the most famous example of 4ths used in a riff is Ritchie Blackmore's intro to *Smoke on the Water*, but they need to be a part of every country rocker's toolkit, and the following examples show some common approaches to using double-stops.

Example 4r uses the G Minor Pentatonic scale (G Bb C D F). A systematic approach to practicing double-stops will help the fingers become accustomed to fretting 4th intervals. Start with the first finger barring the A and D strings at the 3rd fret, then use the third and fourth fingers together to fret at the 5th, while the first finger remains in place. Copy this pattern across the strings.

Example 4r

Unlike the previous example, this phrase features double-stops where the notes move against each other, which demands more work from the fretting hand. In bar one, keep the third finger fretted on the B string throughout and use the second finger for the notes on the G and D strings. In bar two, use the third and fourth fingers at the 5th fret, then move both fingers down to the 3rd before releasing the third finger to sound the open G string against the 3rd fret of the B string.

Example 4s

```
G7
```

```
T|--3----3----0---------3----3----3-----||--5----3----3-----||
A|--0----3----0----0----0----3----0-----||--5----3----0-----||
B|---------------3----------------------||-------------------||
```

Add some rhythm and phrasing to double-stops and riffs begin to emerge. This idea is a Keith Richards-inspired double-stop riff that includes some slides to make it more distinctive. Use the second and third fingers on the D and G strings respectively, making sure you keep the pressure on both fingers as you slide from the 3rd to 2nd fret. When you've played this phrase a few times, try pulling off both fingers to the open strings.

Example 4t

```
G7
```

Next, a Lynyrd Skynyrd-inspired idea. Keep the third finger placed on the 3rd fret of the B string throughout. Use the second finger for the 3rd fret of the B string, and the first finger for the notes that follow on the 2nd fret of the D and G strings. The challenge here comes from the changing rhythms and the fact that the third finger needs to remain fretted while the second finger moves against it.

Example 4u

Chapter Five – Artist Studies 1

In the next two chapters you'll study how some of the legends of country rock guitar shaped the sound of the genre and developed their own approaches, applying the techniques you've learned so far. This chapter focuses on guitarists from two of the southern rock scene's biggest bands: Lynyrd Skynyrd and The Allman Brothers.

Here, you'll learn an example of how each artist approached riff-writing and accompaniment, followed by a series of licks that demonstrate their approach to soloing.

Allen Collins

An original member of Lynyrd Skynyrd, Allen Collins' guitar style is the epitome of the southern rock sound. Collins is perhaps best known for his extended soloing on the classic *Freebird*, a song he co-wrote with vocalist Ronnie Van Zant. He also co-wrote the legendary Skynyrd tracks, *That Smell* and *Gimme Three Steps*. Chunky, open string riffs, and brisk minor pentatonic solos form the bedrock of his style.

The various guitarists in Skynyrd have different approaches to riff-writing but this example highlights the importance of muting, specifically the silences in between the riffs. This means using the palm of the picking hand to stop the strings after you've played each phrase. In bar one, mute the first half of beat 2, and in bar two, mute all of beat 2 and the first part of beat 3. Listen to the audio to get the feel.

Example 5a

Repetition phrasing is a large part of Collin's approach to soloing – just listen to the outro solo in *Freebird* to hear this in action. This A Minor Pentatonic lick can be played with the third finger on the 17th fret of the G string and the first finger on the 14th fret. Listen to how much can be achieved with just a handful of notes and some clever phrasing.

Example 5b

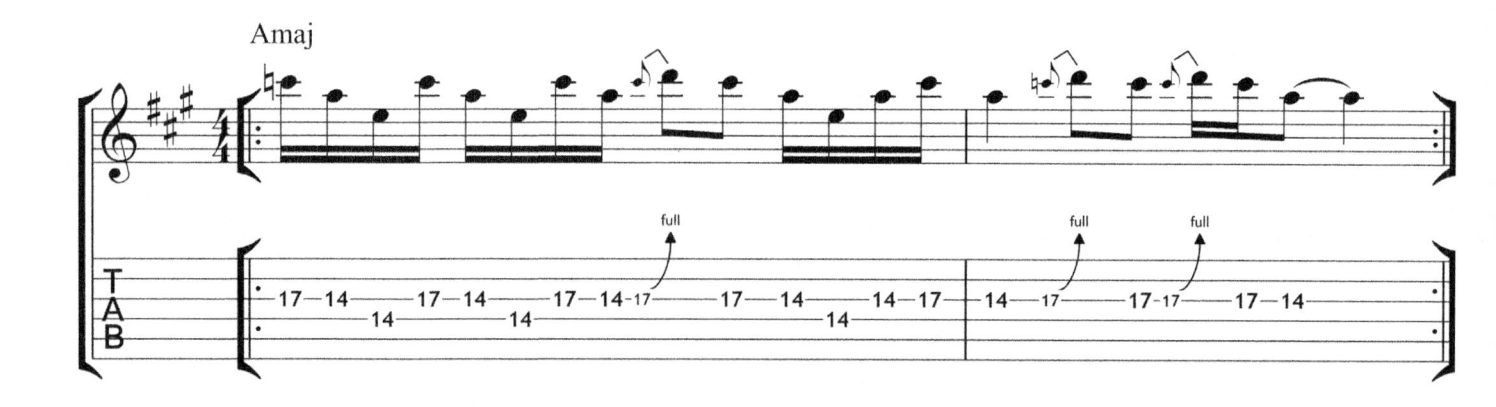

[Musical notation and tablature in A major showing:
Measure 1: 17-14, 17-14, 17-14-17, 17-14, 14-17 (with "full" bend marking); 14 on lower string
Measure 2: 14-17, 17-17, 17-14 with "full" bend markings]

Here's another Collins-style lick using the A Minor Pentatonic scale. Listen to the audio to hear the articulation in this idea. Whole step bends are combined with a fast half step bend, so work hard to get your pitch accuracy on point. Notice that you can loop the entire idea around and keep it going over the backing.

Example 5c

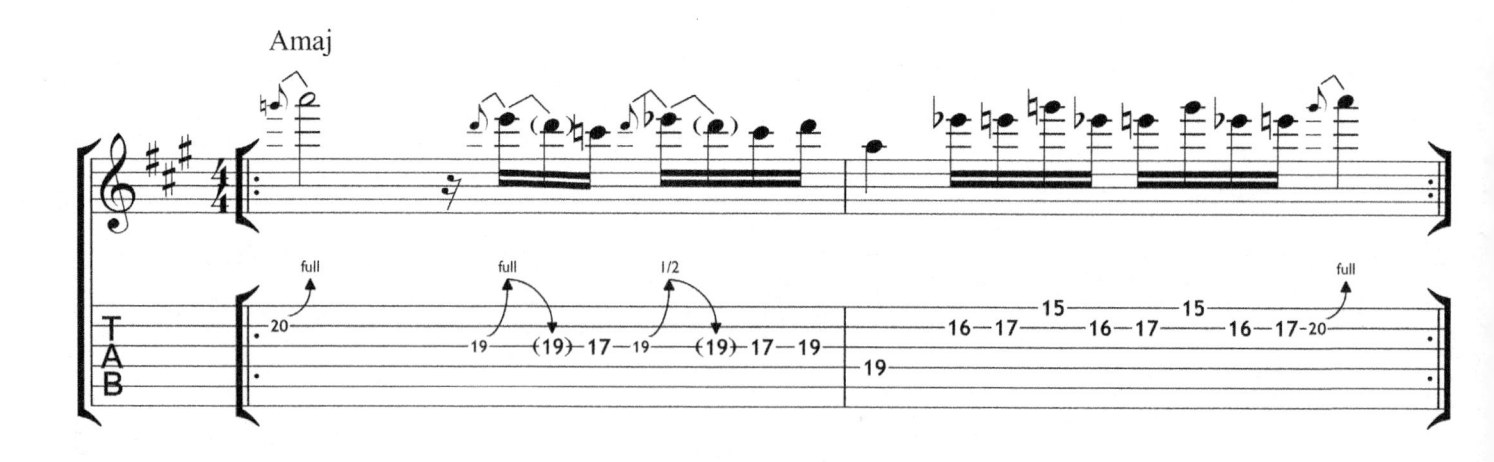

[Musical notation and tablature in A major showing:
Measure 1: 20 (full bend), 19-(19)-17-19 (full bend), (19)-17-19 (1/2 bend)
Measure 2: 16-17-15, 16-17-15, 16-17-20 (full bend); 19 on lower string]

Here's a country inspired A Major Pentatonic lick that uses elements from the string bending chapters you studied earlier. Start with the second finger on the G string at the 11th fret, and follow this with the first then third finger on the B string. Hold the bend in place and use the fourth finger for the high E string, 12th fret. If you're using an overdrive pedal, strive for clean note separation here. We want the notes to ring into each other, but not to become muddy.

Example 5d

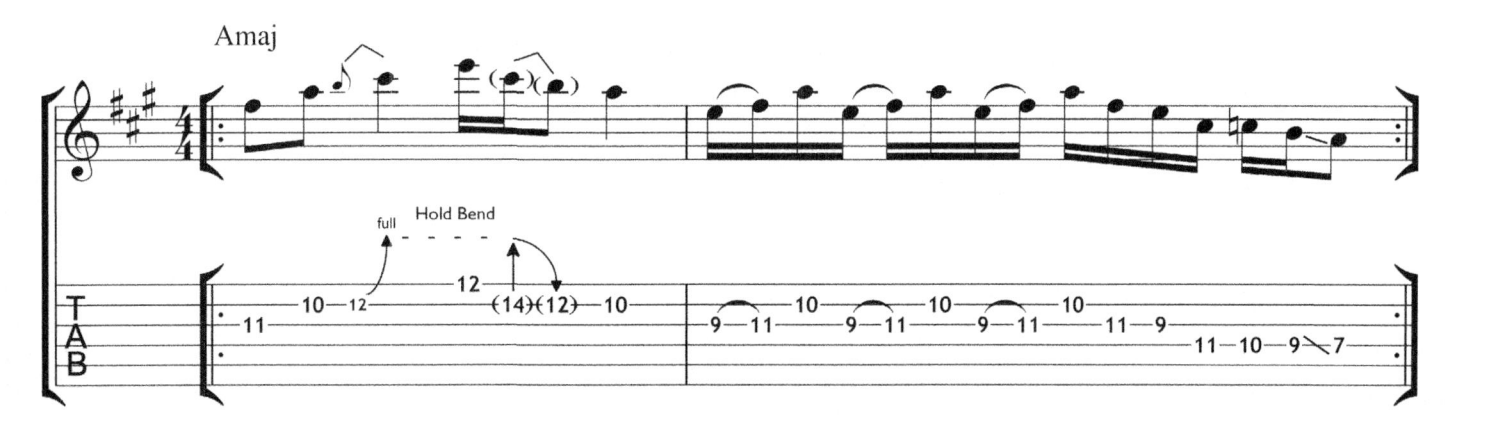

Ed King

Ed King joined Lynyrd Skynyrd initially as a replacement for bassist Leon Wilkeson, but switched to guitar when Wilkeson returned to bass duties. This created the famous three guitar sound and King was soon writing classics like *Sweet Home Alabama* (though it's worth noting that King was the only non-southerner in the band and actually hailed from California!)

The first example requires the cross-picking approach discussed in Chapter One. Jumping from the A string to the B string demands some deft picking hand accuracy. Keep the third and fourth fingers on the 3rd fret of the B and E strings throughout and use the first and second for everything else. Think of the lick as being based around a modified open G chord shape.

Example 5e

This example shows how King might play over the previous example using chord tones and arpeggios to create melodic lines. The main thing to take away from this example is the descending G major arpeggio on beat 4 of bar one. This G major triad in root position outlines the 5th (D), 3rd (B) and root (G) of G major.

Example 5f

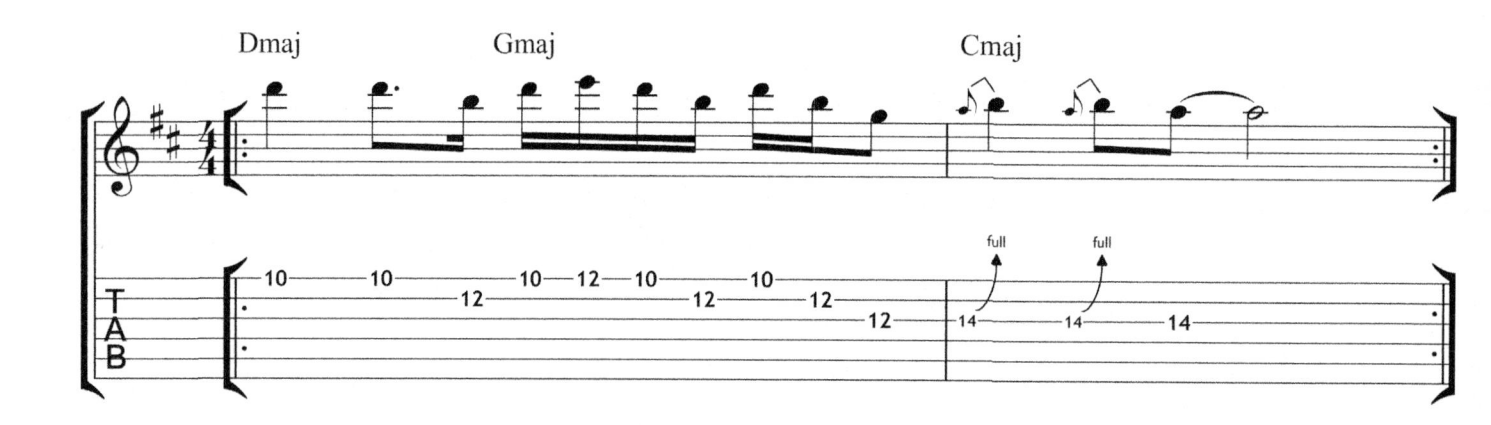

[Musical notation and guitar tab showing Dmaj, Gmaj, Cmaj chords]

Here's another melodic line where King goes beyond pentatonic licks to open with a phrase based around the D Major scale (D E F# G A B C#). Play the legato sequence on beats 1 and 2 with the second finger at the 15th fret and the first finger at the 14th fret. In bar two, try using the second finger for the bend on the B string, as this helps you reach up to the 17th fret of the E string with the fourth finger.

Example 5g

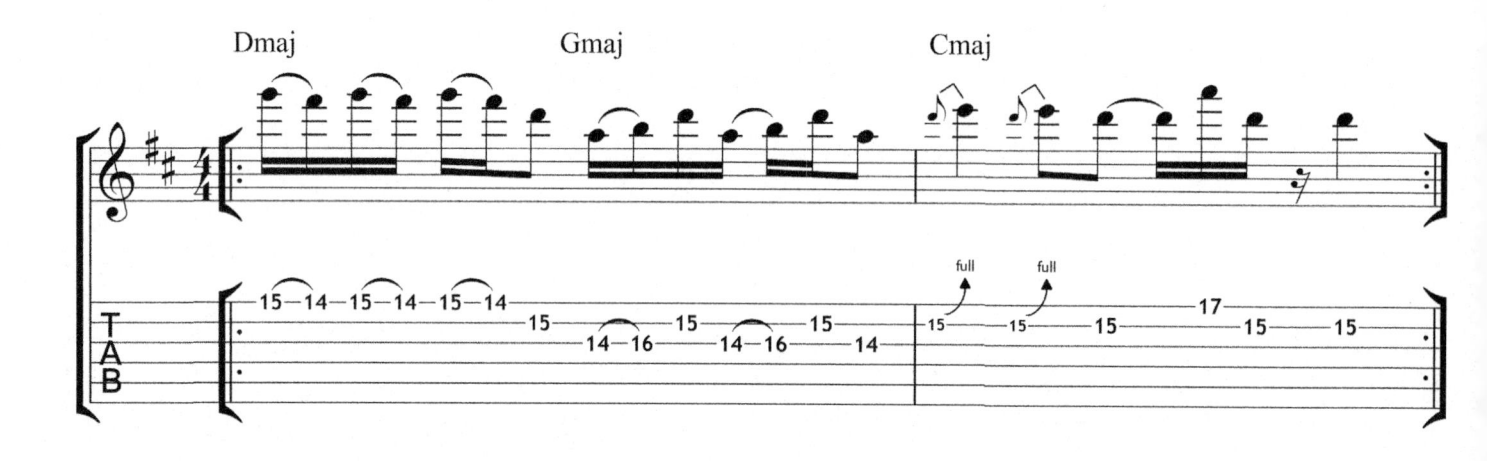

[Musical notation and guitar tab showing Dmaj, Gmaj, Cmaj chords]

Tasteful D Major Pentatonic licks open this phrase with a strong awareness of "common tones", i.e. notes that different chords share. In this case, the D on the 10th fret of the E string is the root of the D major and the 5th of the G major chord. Bar two features a return to the D Major scale and more legato.

Example 5h

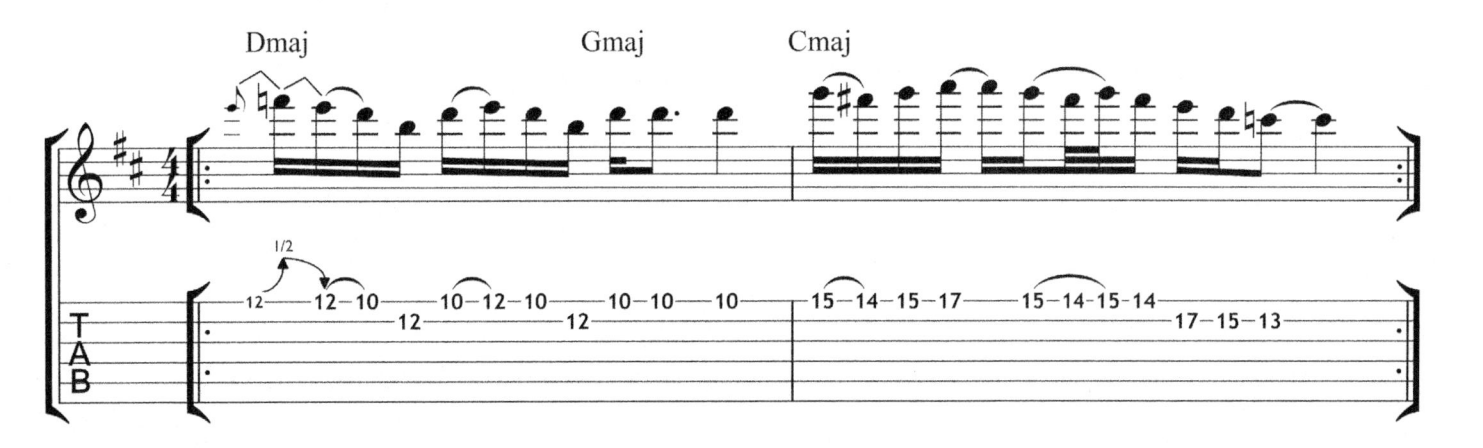

Gary Rossington

A founder member of Lynyrd Skynyrd, Gary Rossington was influenced by Duane Allman, Jimi Hendrix and particularly Eric Clapton. He developed his own style though, and his licks with Skynyrd are a masterclass in chord tones, melodic phrasing and the blues-meets-country approach common to this style.

Here is a Rossington-style picked line. If you are new to the 6/8 meter, it's important to feel this time signature correctly. Some people feel it as two beats in the bar with each beat having a triplet feel. Others find it easier to count, "1 2 3 4 5 6" for each bar. Check out the audio and try both counting methods to see which you prefer.

To play the F# in bar three, hook the thumb over the 2nd fret of the low E string and use the third finger on the 5th string and the fourth finger on the D string.

Example 5i

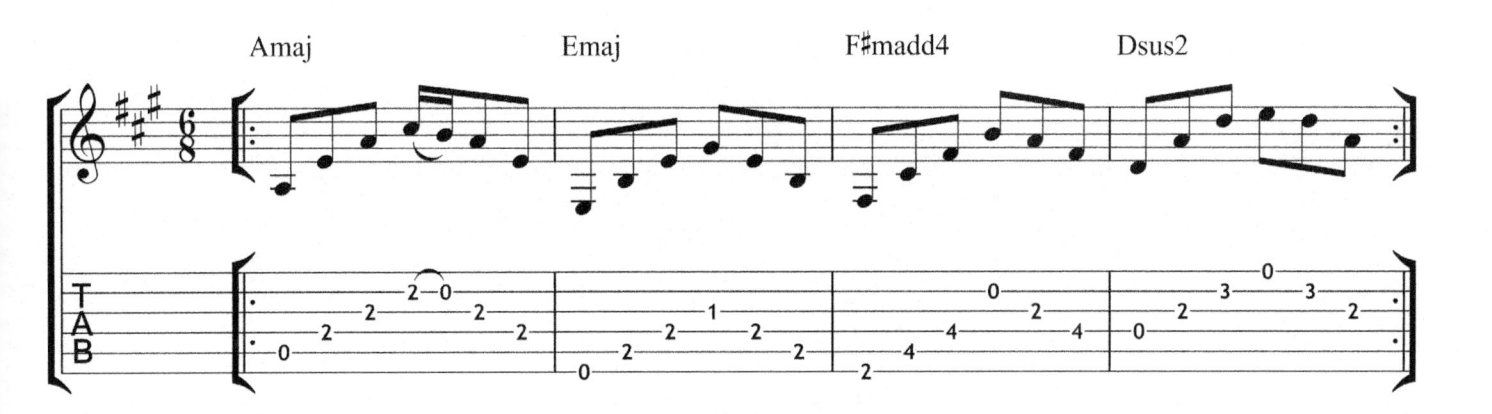

This lick uses the A Major scale (A B C# D E F# G#) to create a melodic part that contrasts space in the first two bars with a longer line in bars 3-4. When playing like this, aim to use the scale to target the notes in the chords you are soloing over. For example, over the E major chord in bar two, the E root note is highlighted and the G# on the B string, 9th fret, is the 3rd.

Example 5j

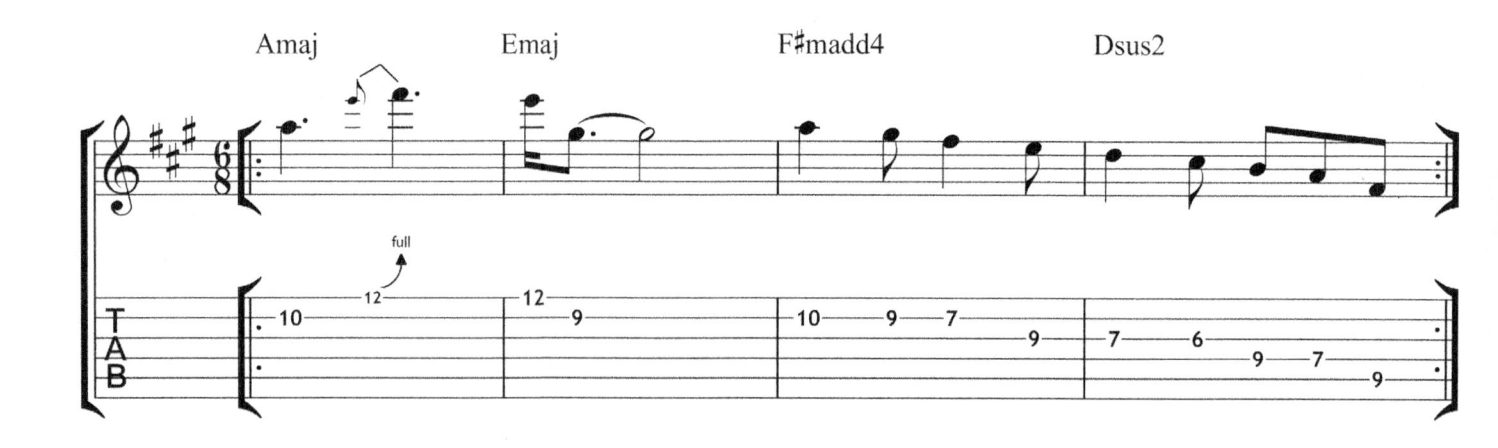

Here's an example of Rossington's beautiful phrasing and motif building. Make sure your pitching is accurate in each bar and focus on the repeated bend and release in the final bar.

Example 5k

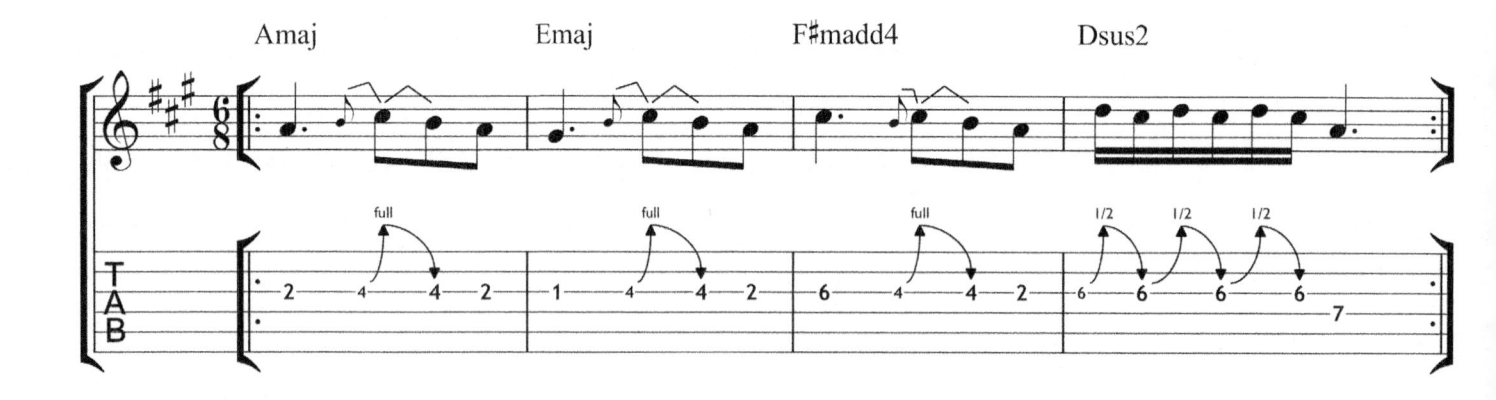

You can get a lot of mileage out of simple pentatonic scales. In the first two bars, a motif is created from the A Major Pentatonic scale (A B C# E F#). To create motifs like this, simply repeat an idea over the next chord but aim to end the lick on a chord tone of the new chord.

Example 5l

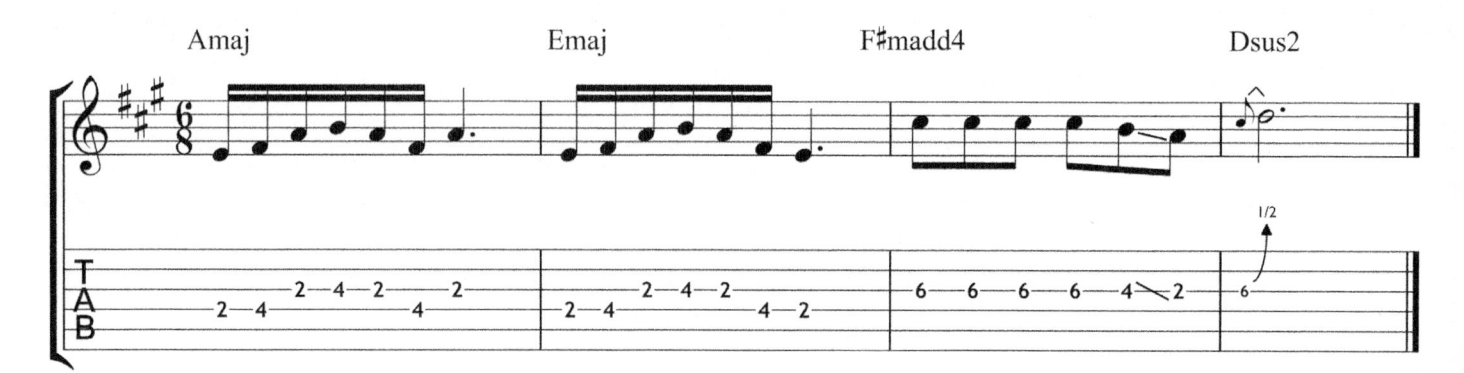

Duane Allman

One of the greatest guitarists of all time, it's remarkable how much Duane Allman achieved before his tragic death at just 24 years of age. A seasoned session player and founder of The Allman Brothers, Duane had performed and recorded with soul stars Wilson Pickett and Aretha Franklin, and that's his slide playing on Eric Clapton's classic *Layla*. Even more sobering is the fact that he had only been playing slide guitar for three years before his death.

Triads (simple three-note chords comprising the root, third and fifth of a scale) were a common feature of Allman Brothers rhythm parts. Triads are perfect when dealing with fast moving chord progressions because they are easy to move around the neck, plus they don't take up much sonic space in a band mix, compared to barre chords, which allows them to cut through.

Example 5m

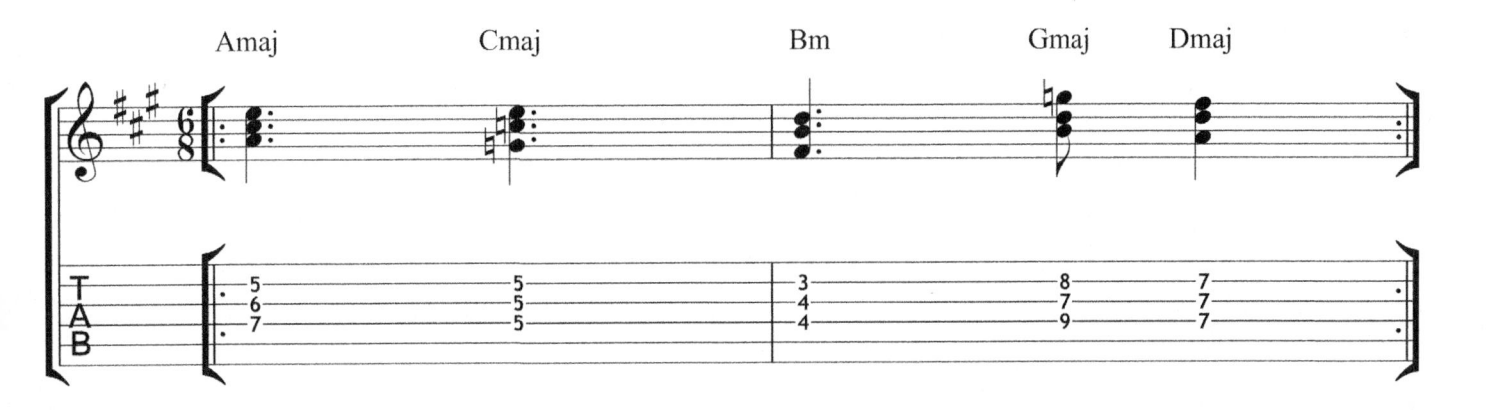

This first example lick examines Duane's soloing style without the slide, where jazz influenced lines collide with the blues. Duane was a huge fan of jazz legends Miles Davis and John Coltrane, and this is an example of his long, flowing lines. The lick is based around the A Minor Pentatonic scale (A C D E G) with a B note added over the C major chord in bar one. The last three notes of bar spell an E minor triad (E G B) superimposed over the C major chord, which creates the sound of a C major 7 arpeggio (C E G B).

Example 5n

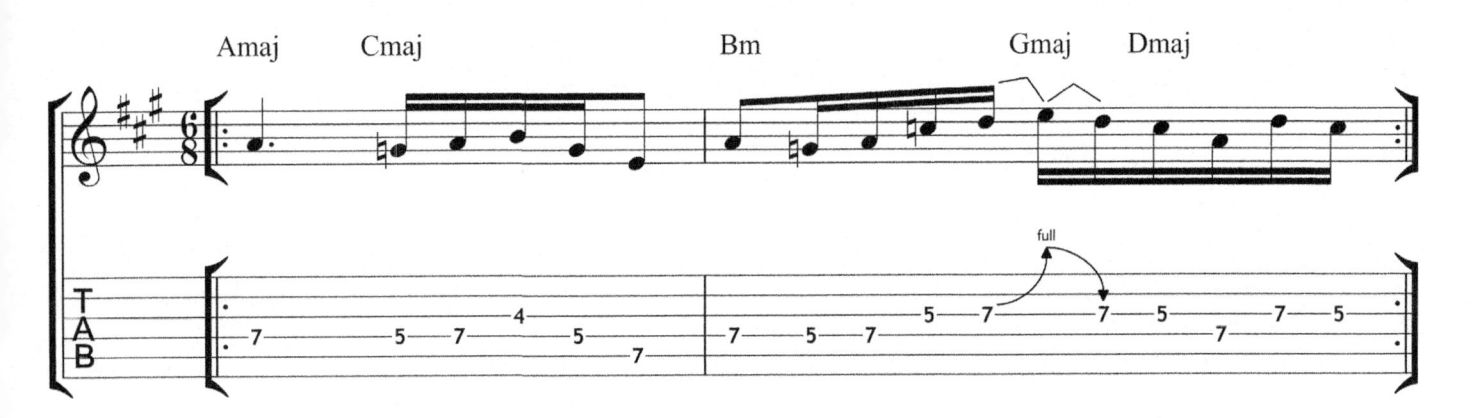

Here's another example of Duane's arpeggio superimposition approach. In this case, the lick begins with a G major triad inversion (D G B). Played over the A major backing, it implies the sound of an A11 chord. This "chord on chord" approach helped Duane break out of minor pentatonic licks to create his ultra-melodic lead sound.

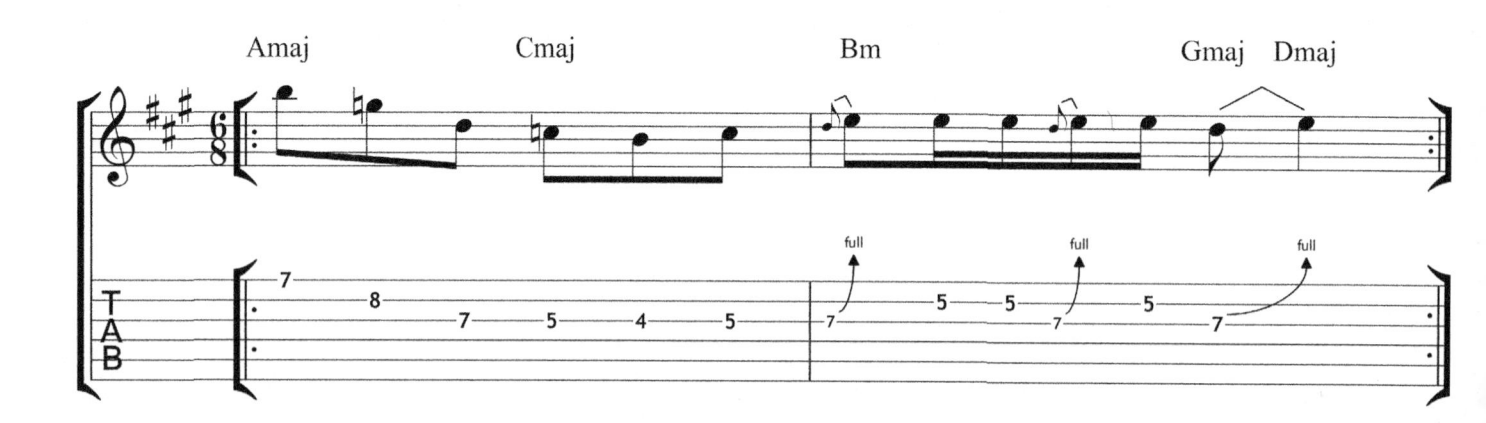

Example 5o

The flowing, jazz influence is in evidence again here. This lick is based around the A Blues scale (A C D Eb E G) in bar one and, as is common in jazz, additional chromatic passing notes (notes that don't belong to the key) have been added to create a continuous line. This idea can really open up the sound of your licks but use it in moderation!

Example 5p

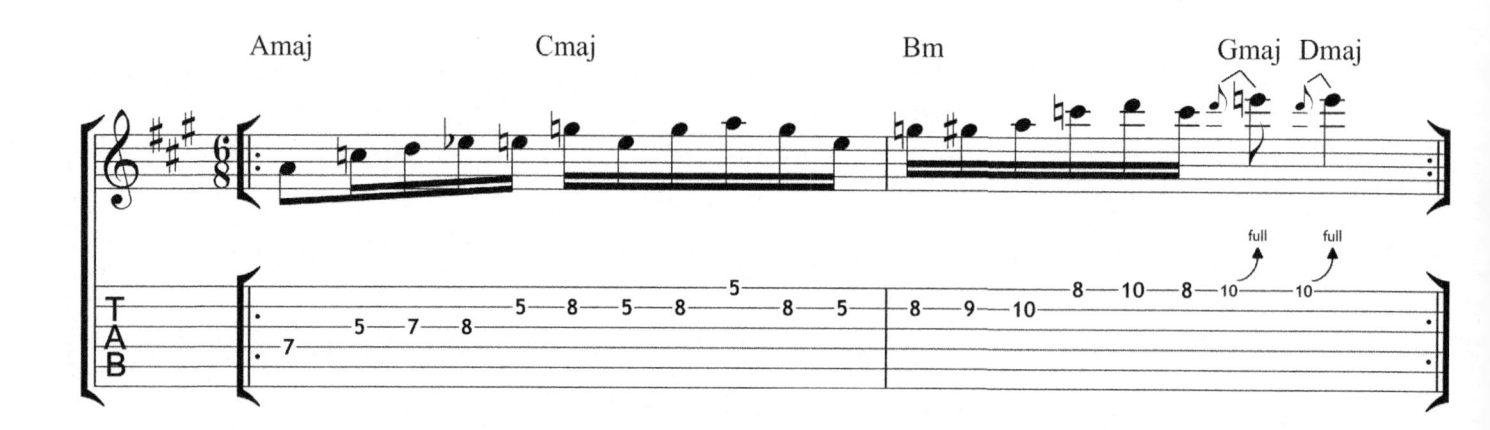

Dickey Betts

A founding member of The Allman Brothers, Dickey Betts helped shape the sound of country rock guitar with his six-string partner, Duane Allman, and the pair brought twin guitar harmony to the fore. Following Duane's tragic death in 1971, Betts became the band's only lead guitarist. A highly melodic player, his flowing lines on instrumentals like *Jessica* and *In Memory of Elizabeth Reed* made him one of the most influential players in genre.

Triads on the D, G and B strings are a great tool for outlining the harmony while not getting in the way of the bass or piano. Bar one uses a common E major to A major movement. Barre with the first finger at the 9th fret for the E chord. Use the second and third fingers to play the A chord with the barre still in place. On the fretboard it looks like you are hammering onto an F#m chord.

For the B chord in bar two, use the first finger on the B string and let the second/third fingers fall naturally onto the G/D strings. To change to the E major chord quickly, just flatten the third finger across the 9th fret.

Example 5q

Betts often added an extra note to a five-note pentatonic scale to form a six-note (hexatonic) scale. In this example, the E Major Pentatonic scale (E F# G# B C#) has an A note added, which is played on the B string, 10th fret.

Example 5r

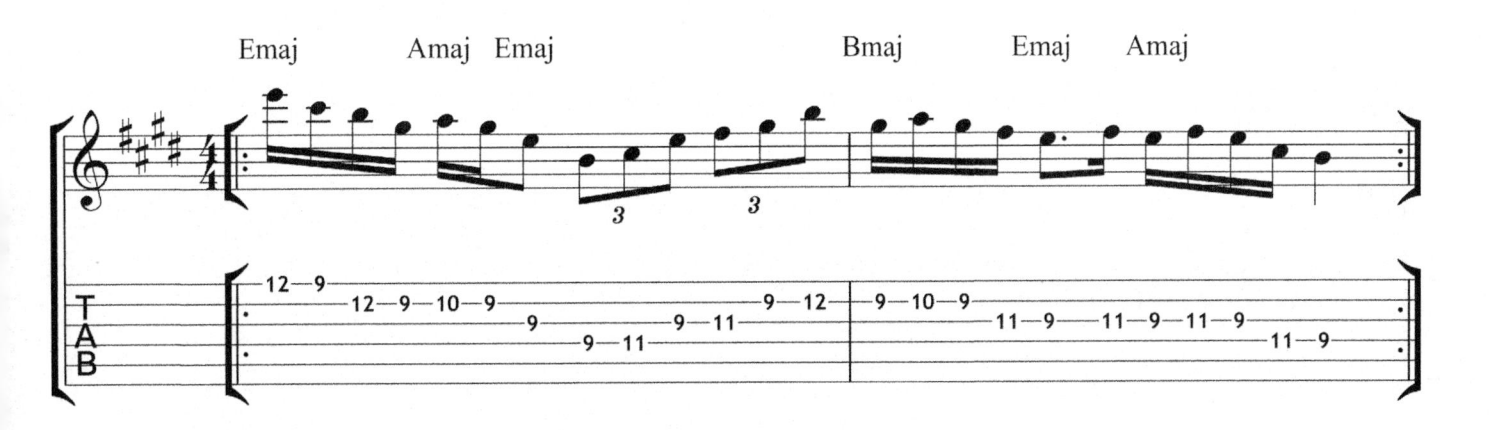

Hexatonic scales make Bett's phrases more melodic and that extra note allows him to create stronger lines. Listen to the melodic character that is added by this one carefully placed A note.

Example 5s

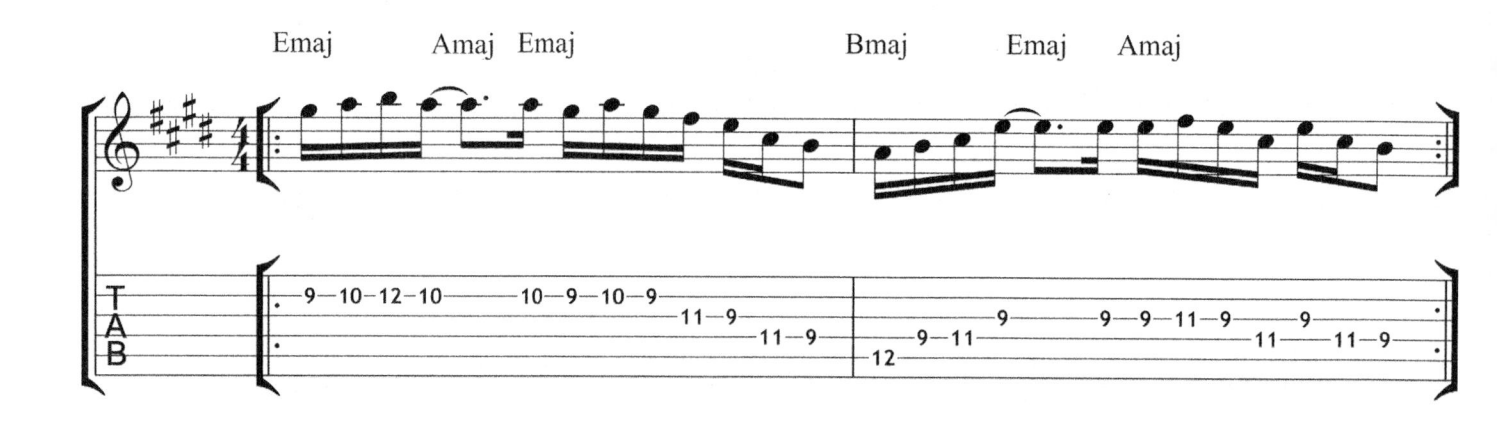

[Guitar tablature in E major, 4/4 time. Chords: Emaj, Amaj, Emaj, Bmaj, Emaj, Amaj]

```
Bar 1: 9-10-12-10, 10-9-10-9, 11-9, 11-9
Bar 2: 12, 9-11, 9, 9-9-11-9, 9, 11, 11-9
```

The hexatonic scale means we have more options for targeting chords. In this example, the added A note is used to target the root of the A chord at the end of bar two.

Example 5t

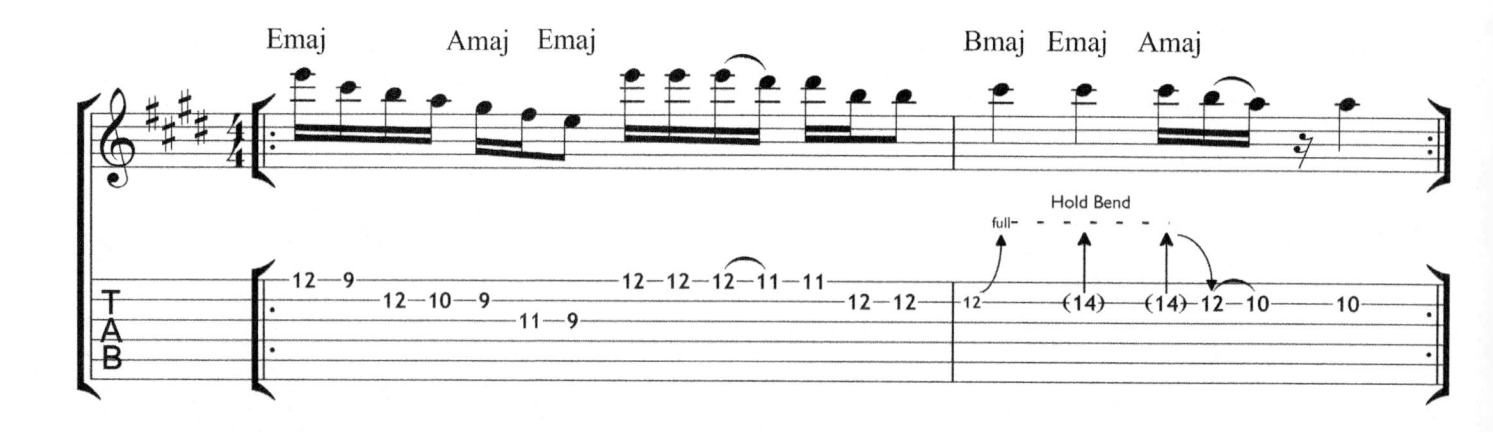

[Guitar tablature in E major, 4/4 time. Chords: Emaj, Amaj, Emaj, Bmaj, Emaj, Amaj. Includes full bend and Hold Bend notations]

```
Bar 1: 12-9, 12-10-9, 11-9, 12-12-12-11-11
Bar 2: 12-12, 12, (14), (14)-12-10, 10
```

We've looked at the styles of some of the heroes of southern rock. In the next chapter we'll explore the Laurel Canyon sound of the west coast.

Chapter Six – Artist Studies 2

While the southern scene was busy creating one strand of country rock, on the west coast of the US the LA/Laurel Canyon sound was developing its own. The dawn of this style came via the music of bands like The Byrds and Buffalo Springfield, and the 1970s saw the arrival of The Eagles and Creedence Clearwater Revival. Meanwhile, The Rolling Stones were busy developing the country rock element in their music and, later on, artists like Tom Petty and James Taylor would also incorporate this sound into their writing.

The LA/Laurel Canyon sound tends to be softer than southern country rock but is just as melodic. In this chapter, you'll study some of the key players from this scene and learn how they created their riffs and licks.

Buffalo Springfield/The Byrds

The late 1960s Laurel Canyon sound of The Byrds and Buffalo Springfield gave birth to the sound of LA country rock. Buffalo Springfield guitarists Neil Young and Stephen Stills melded acoustic and electric guitars, while The Byrds featured Gram Parsons and bluegrass/country legend Clarence White. Principal Byrds songwriters Roger McGuinn and Gene Parsons explored the sound of American country and added the harder sound of 1960s rock.

This example explores the jangly sound of 1960s guitar that would become a feature of this brand of country rock. Notice that this picked arpeggio passage has the chords arranged on the top four strings, allowing them to cut through and thus avoid any muddiness in the mix. In bands that featured more than one guitar player, this approach was an essential arranging device that left space for other parts.

Example 6a

The '60s-influenced country licks in this example are reminiscent of Stephen Stills and Clarence White. The phrases are drawn from the E Major Pentatonic scale. While you may be familiar with that scale in a blues context, here it is the phrasing that adds the country twist, with bends, legato and rapid-fire rhythms. You can play all of this with the first and third fingers.

Example 6b

The next lick begins with an E Major Pentatonic phrase before moving into country-style 6th intervals for a Clarence White sound. You can play this lick entirely with the pick or hybrid pick it. The pick will strike the G string while the middle finger plucks the E string.

Example 6c

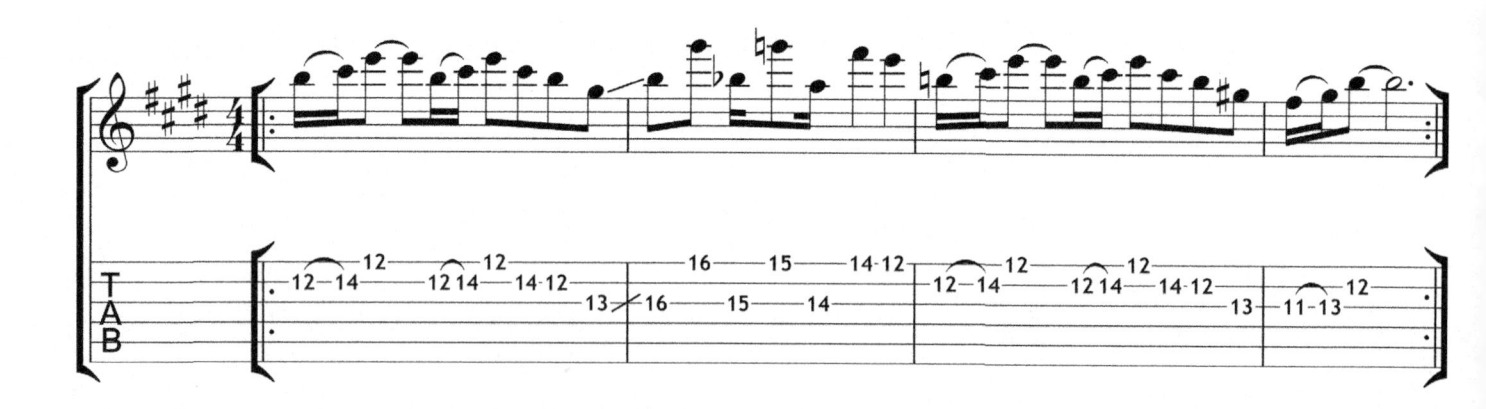

This example shows that the E Major Pentatonic scale can be all you need to play some convincing country rock! With some careful phrasing, bends and string skipping, all these country licks are contained within those five notes. Start this one with the third finger bending the 11th fret of the G string, followed by the fourth finger at the 12th fret of the E string.

Example 6d

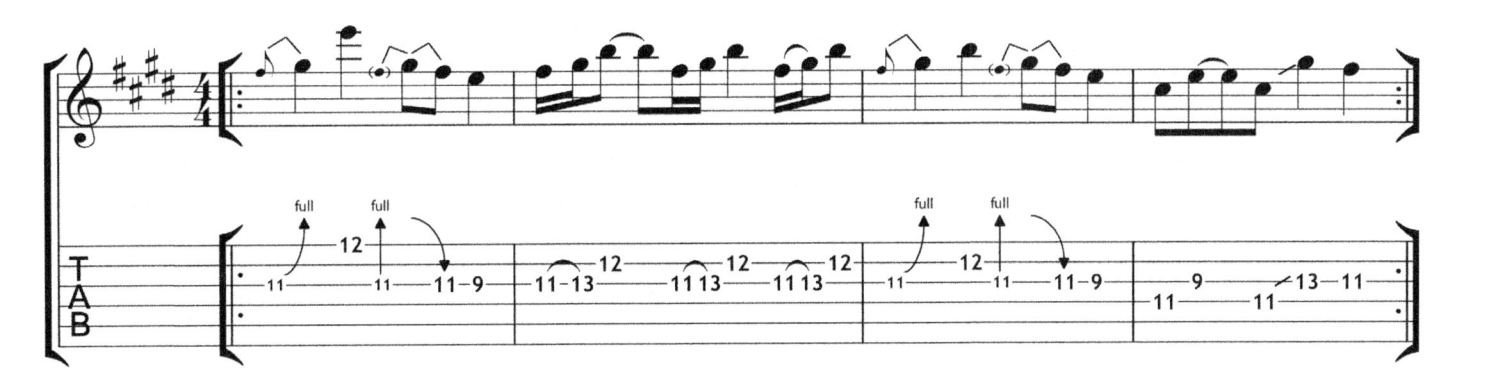

Joe Walsh

Prior to finding superstardom in The Eagles, Joe Walsh had built his reputation in The James Gang and as a solo artist. Joe's style is a musical gumbo of blues, funk, soul and, of course, country. Working in a trio format in The James Gang meant that he needed to cover rhythm and lead duties, and his creative, angular note choices makes him a unique player within the country rock genre.

Joe's rhythm parts often use triads and he will typically play these shapes on the 4th, 3rd and 2nd strings, sometimes using a pedal tone against them, as in this example that makes use of the open A string. Joe will let chords ring while palm muting the open string for a chunky sounding rhythm part.

Example 6e

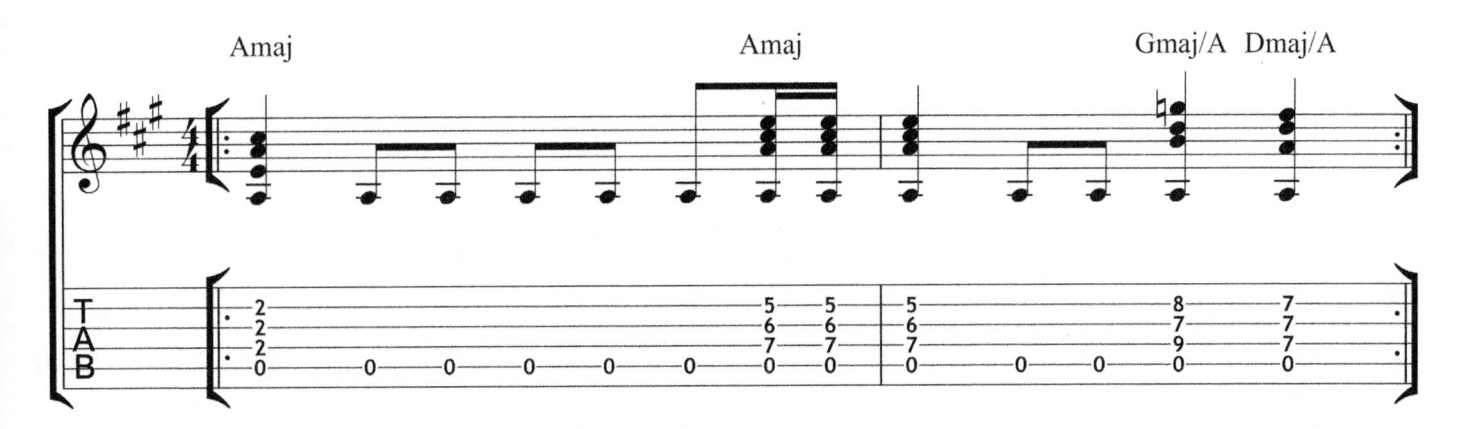

The next example shows what Joe might typically play over that backing. The lick is built from the A Major Pentatonic scale. Playing low on the neck makes the string bends more of a challenge, so use the third finger to play the opening bend on the 4th fret of the G string, with the second finger behind for reinforcement. Use the first finger for the 2nd fret of the E string, followed by the fourth finger at the 5th fret of the B string.

Example 6f

By contrast, this A Major Pentatonic idea is played in the higher register. Joe's note choice is far less predictable than his contemporaries, so it's good to plan how to finger the lick beforehand. Use the first finger on the 14th fret of the E string, the fourth finger on the 17th fret of the B string, and the third finger on the G string, 16th fret. The latter is a pre-bend, so remember to push the string up before playing!

Example 6g

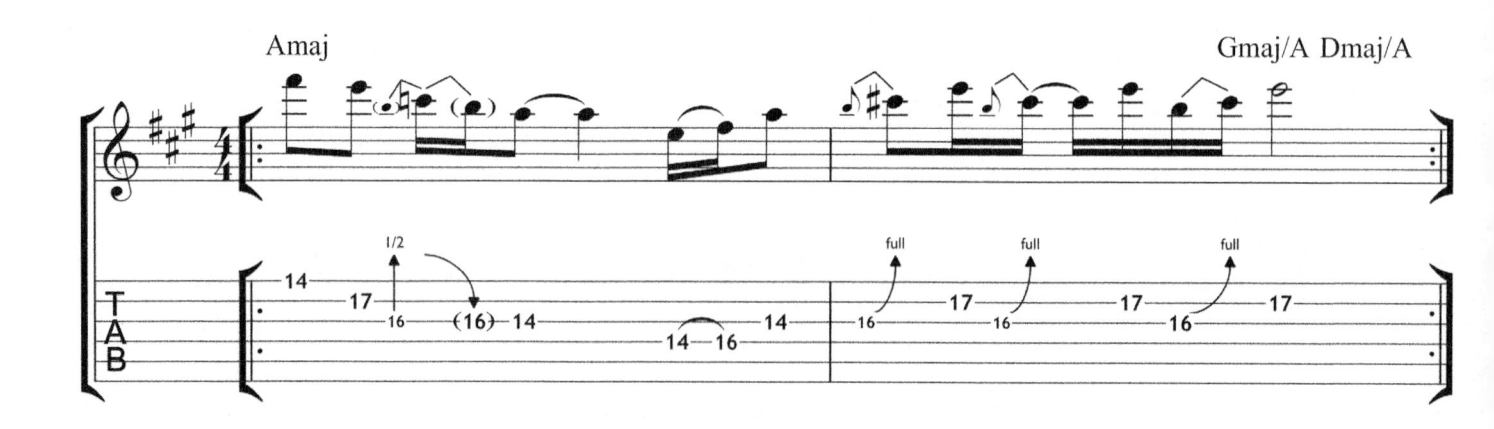

One of the coolest aspects of Joe's playing is his use of chromatic passing notes, which add a lot of spice to a line if used carefully. This line uses the A Major Pentatonic scale as its framework but a b5 passing note is added (Eb) along with a minor 3rd (C). Together, the note choices result in a cool, dark country blues sound.

Example 6h

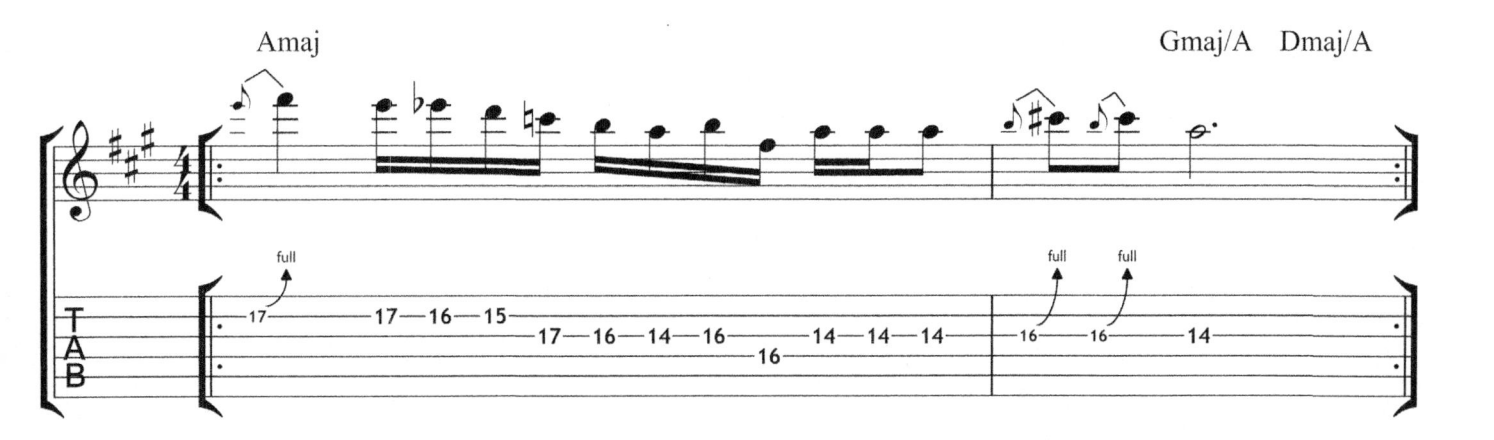

Don Felder

When The Eagles began to move away from their country roots in pursuit of a rockier sound, Don Felder was the guitarist they chose to pair with Joe Walsh. Felder had actually known Eagles' founding member Bernie Leadon from a young age and had played with Walsh over the years, so was a perfect fit. His playing introduced a harder-edged rock sound, but of course his style was still full of country rock traits from the string bends to note choice.

Felder is perhaps most famous for his chordal work on the intro to *Hotel California* and his approach to chords in general brought a new sound to the band. Instead of simple major and minor chords, this example uses richer sounding major 7, minor 9 and minor 7 chords. The rhythms played are more sophisticated too, moving beyond simple country strumming patterns to introduce a much funkier sound. Keep the strumming hand loose and focus on timing here.

Example 6i

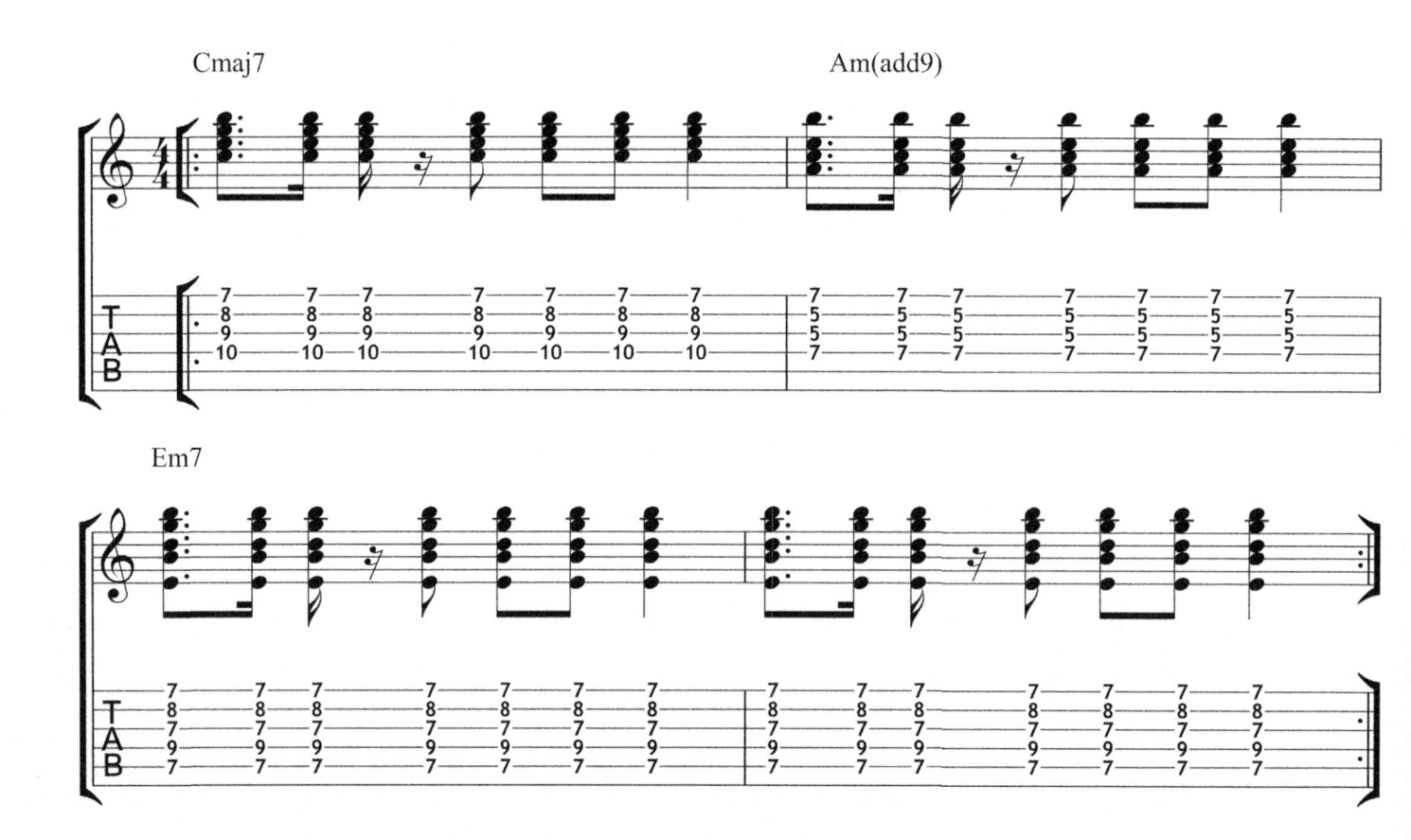

Felder's blues-rock inspired licks are a masterclass in motifs – phrases based around coherent, repetitive musical ideas. This lick uses the E Minor Pentatonic scale (E G A B D) and the first two beats of each bar use the same rhythm (two 1/4 notes).

Example 6j

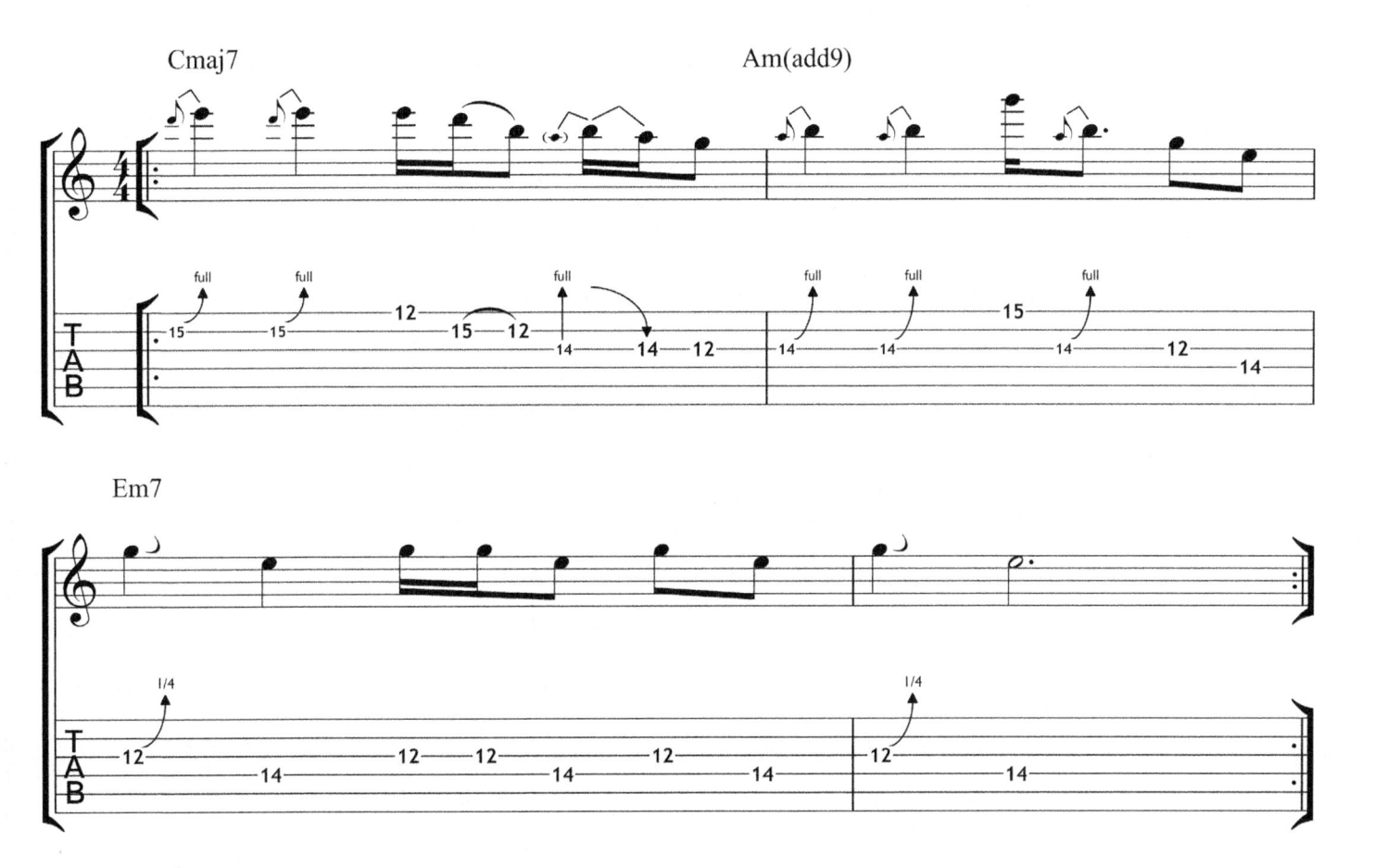

This rock-influenced E Minor Pentatonic scale lick demonstrates Felder's mastery of motifs and repetition with the opening lick repeated in bar two. Start with the third finger for the bend on the E string, then use the first finger at the 17th fret. Use the third or fourth finger for the 20th fret on the B string and the first finger for the 17th fret.

Example 6k

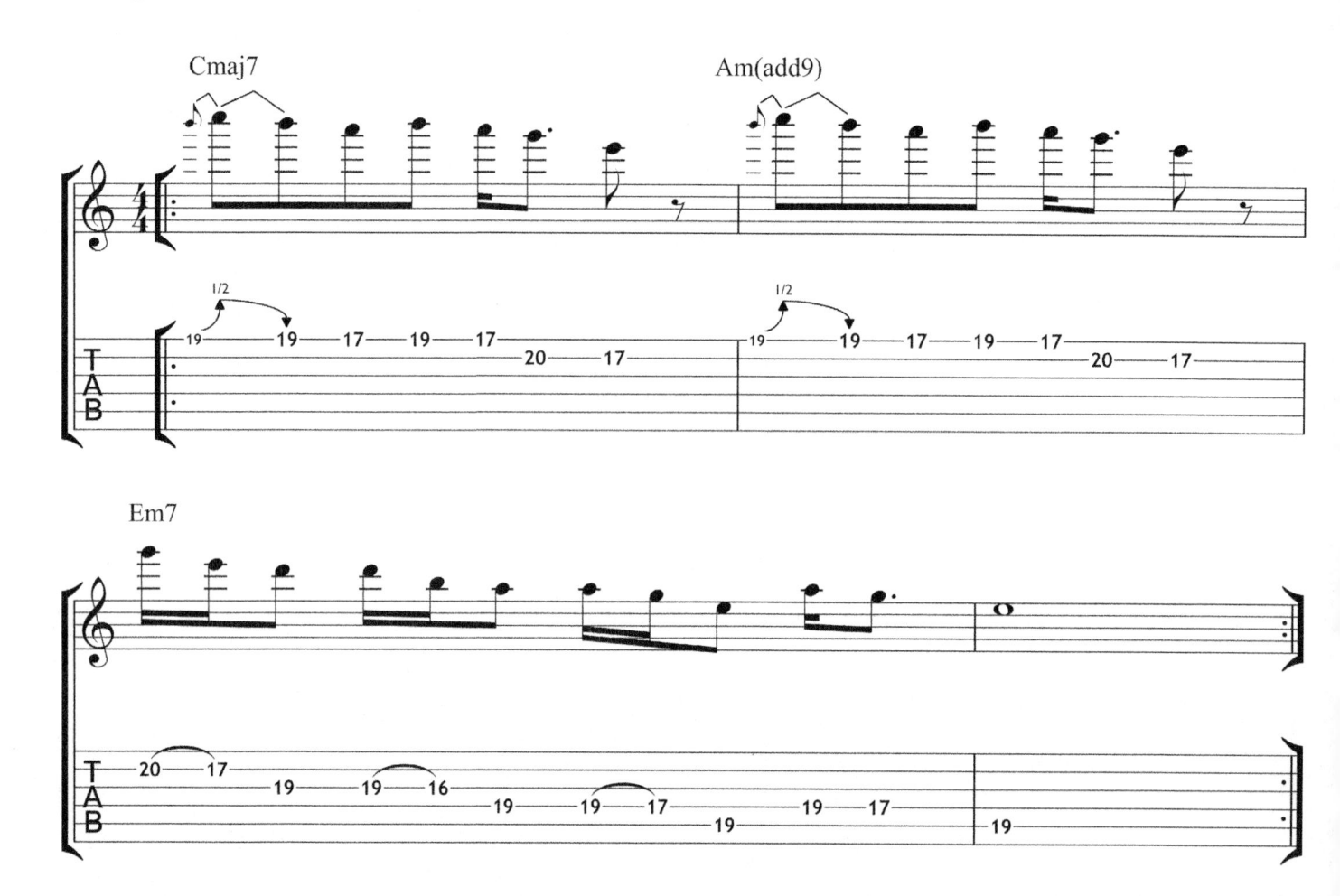

The motif approach is used in a more sophisticated manner here, as the phrase in bar one is slightly modified in bar two. Play the slide from the 14th to 16th fret with the second finger. Use the third finger for the B string, 17th fret, and the first finger for the E string, 15th fret.

Example 61

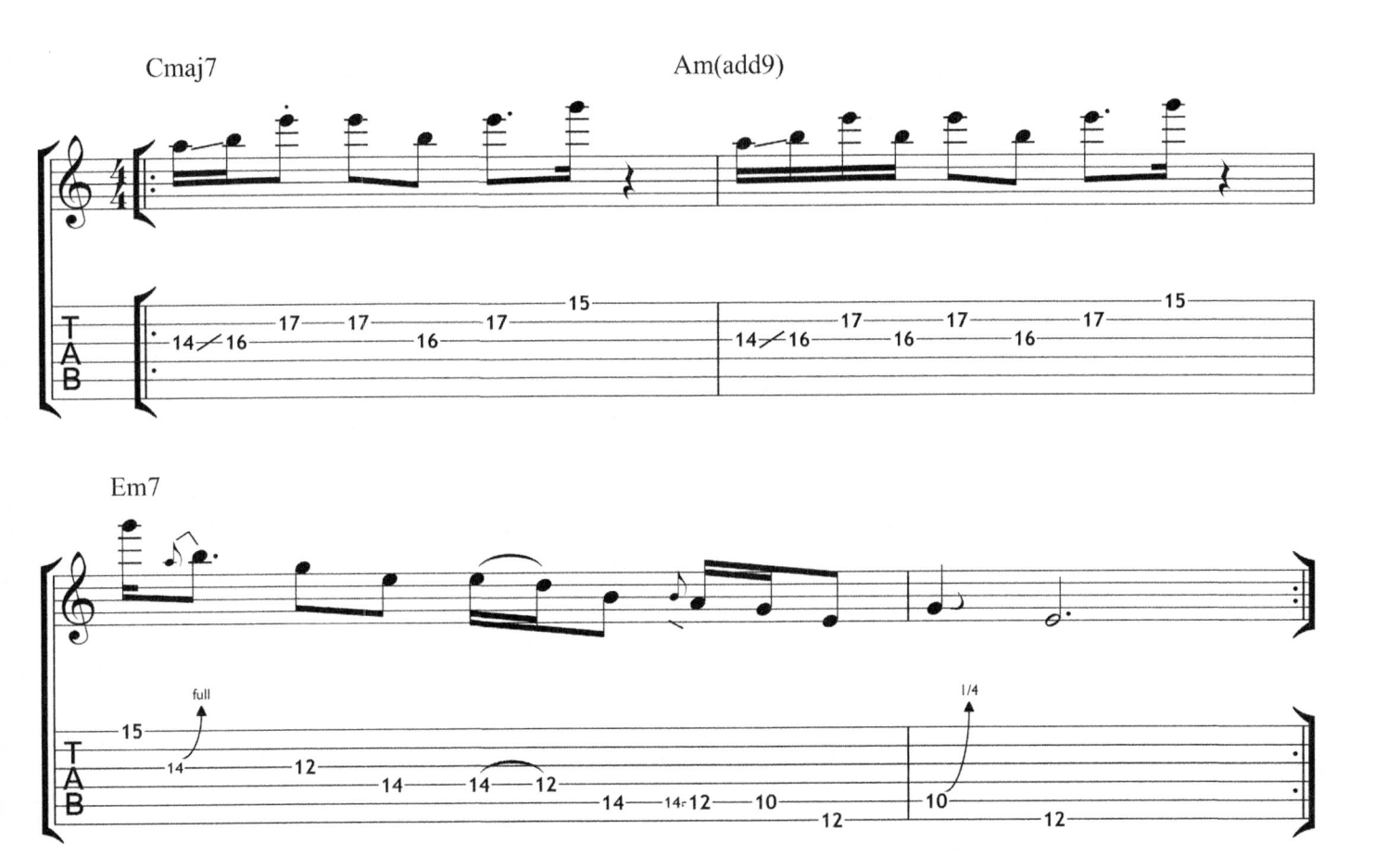

Glenn Frey

A founder-member of The Eagles, Glenn Frey is usually thought of as a songwriter rather than a guitarist, but prior to the arrival of Joe Walsh and Don Felder he would take bluesy, pentatonic-based lead breaks and created parts with interesting chord voicings. His soloing style is more 1960s rock than country, but is still worth studying.

Frey adds character to chord progressions by using interesting voicings. In this example, the top two strings are played open against each chord. This adds much more colour to otherwise routine major and minor voicings.

Example 6m

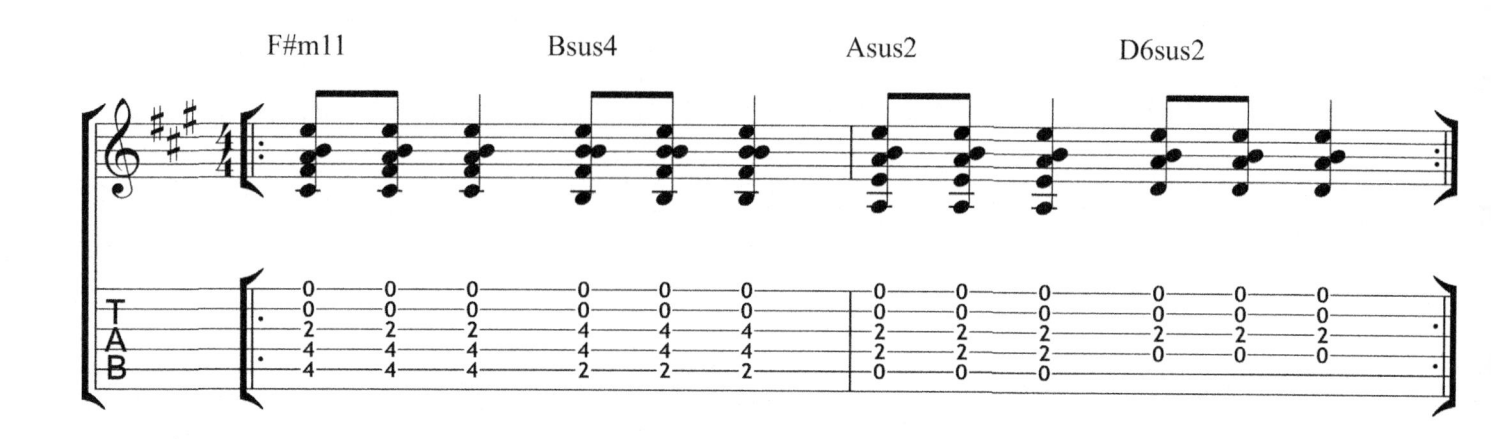

[Musical notation and tablature for Example 6m with chords F#m11, Bsus4, Asus2, D6sus2]

Frey's lead work doesn't feature as many country rock inflections as Walsh and Felder, but he still had great ideas like this F# Minor Pentatonic (F# A B C# E) lick.

Example 6n

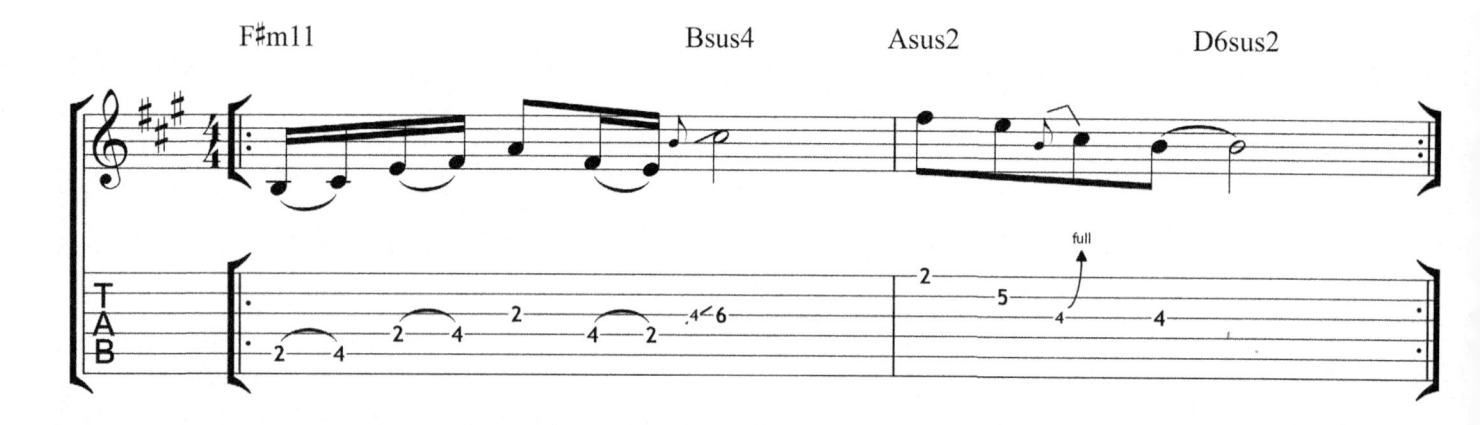

[Musical notation and tablature for Example 6n with chords F#m11, Bsus4, Asus2, D6sus2]

Contrasting space with busier lines is a hallmark of Frey's lead style. This lick is all about targeting the F# note on the 4th fret of the D string. In bar one he hangs onto this note for three beats, then in bar two contrasts this with a run up and down the F# Minor Pentatonic scale before returning to the F#. The scale run can be achieved using just the first and third fingers.

Example 6o

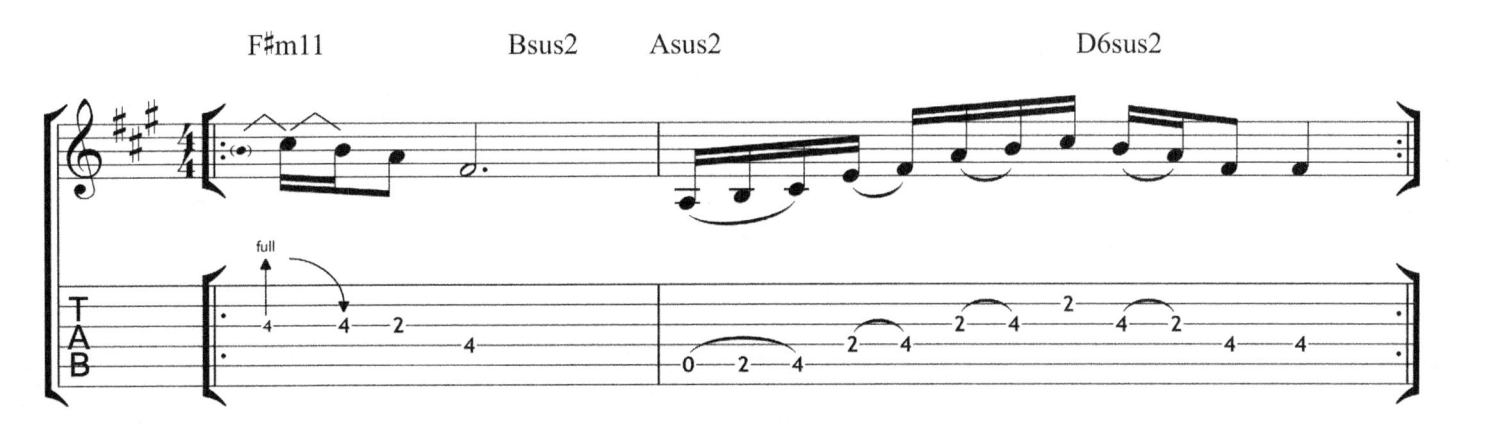

[Musical notation and tab for Example 6o with chords F#m11, Bsus2, Asus2, D6sus2]

While the pentatonic scale was at the core of Frey's lead style, he could be more creative too. This lick is based on a variety of intervals played over each chord and the end result is melodic and cohesive. Working like this really makes you think about what you are playing and using fewer notes means that everything counts. The general guideline is to aim for the defining tones of each chord (root, third, fifth).

Example 6p

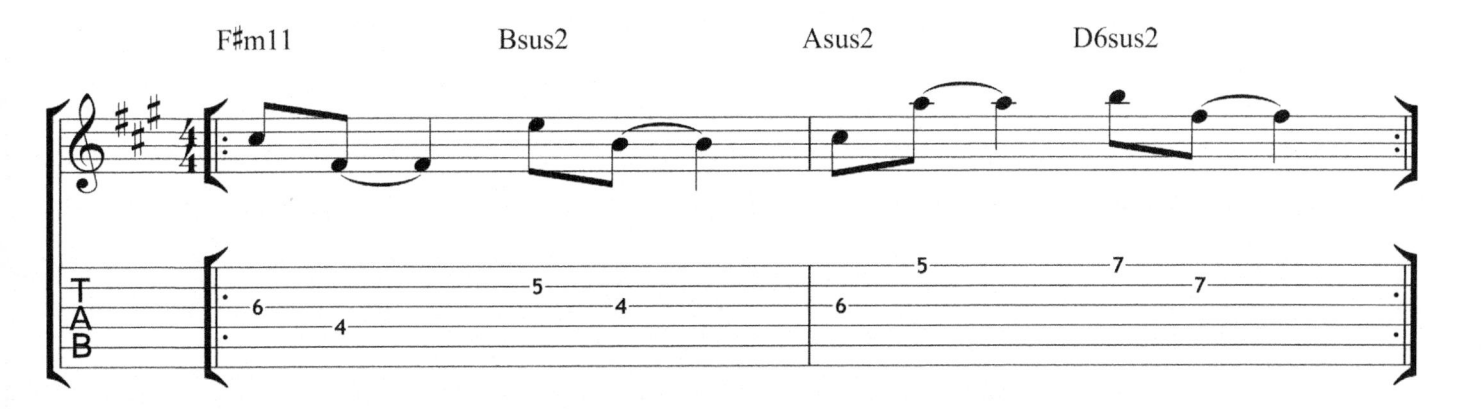

[Musical notation and tab for Example 6p with chords F#m11, Bsus2, Asus2, D6sus2]

Bernie Leadon

Another founder-member of The Eagles, Bernie Leadon was as much a country musician as a rock musician. In addition to guitar, he played banjo, mandolin, Dobro and steel guitar. Listen to the pedal steel style triple-stop bend on the intro to *Take It Easy* to hear his country chops.

Early Eagles music contained a strong country influence, and this lightly swung acoustic rhythm guitar part harks back to legends like Hank Williams and Johnny Cash. At the heart of this idea is the alternating bassline. In bar three, you can either move the third finger from the A string to the E string, or you can finger the C chord with the third finger on the A string and the fourth finger on the E string.

Example 6q

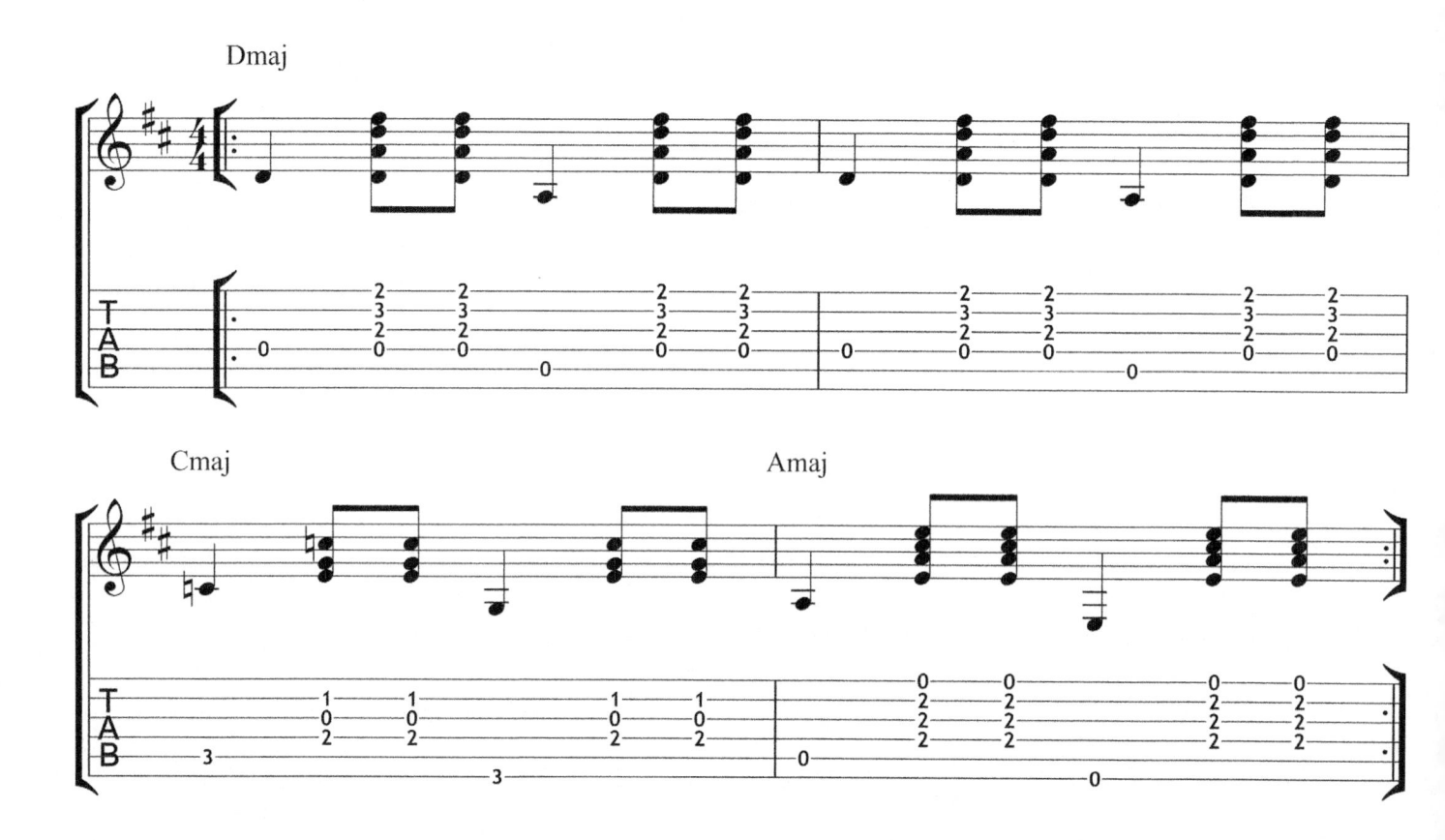

Bernie Leadon's solos always sound well thought out and feature repeating motifs. For the double-stop in bar one, fret the B string, 3rd fret with the second finger, and G string, 2nd fret with the first finger. Use the fourth finger to play the quick hammer-on to the 4th fret.

There is some clever chord tone work in bars 3-4. The notes on the A string move from the root note of C major in bar three to C# (the 3rd of A major) in bar four.

Example 6r

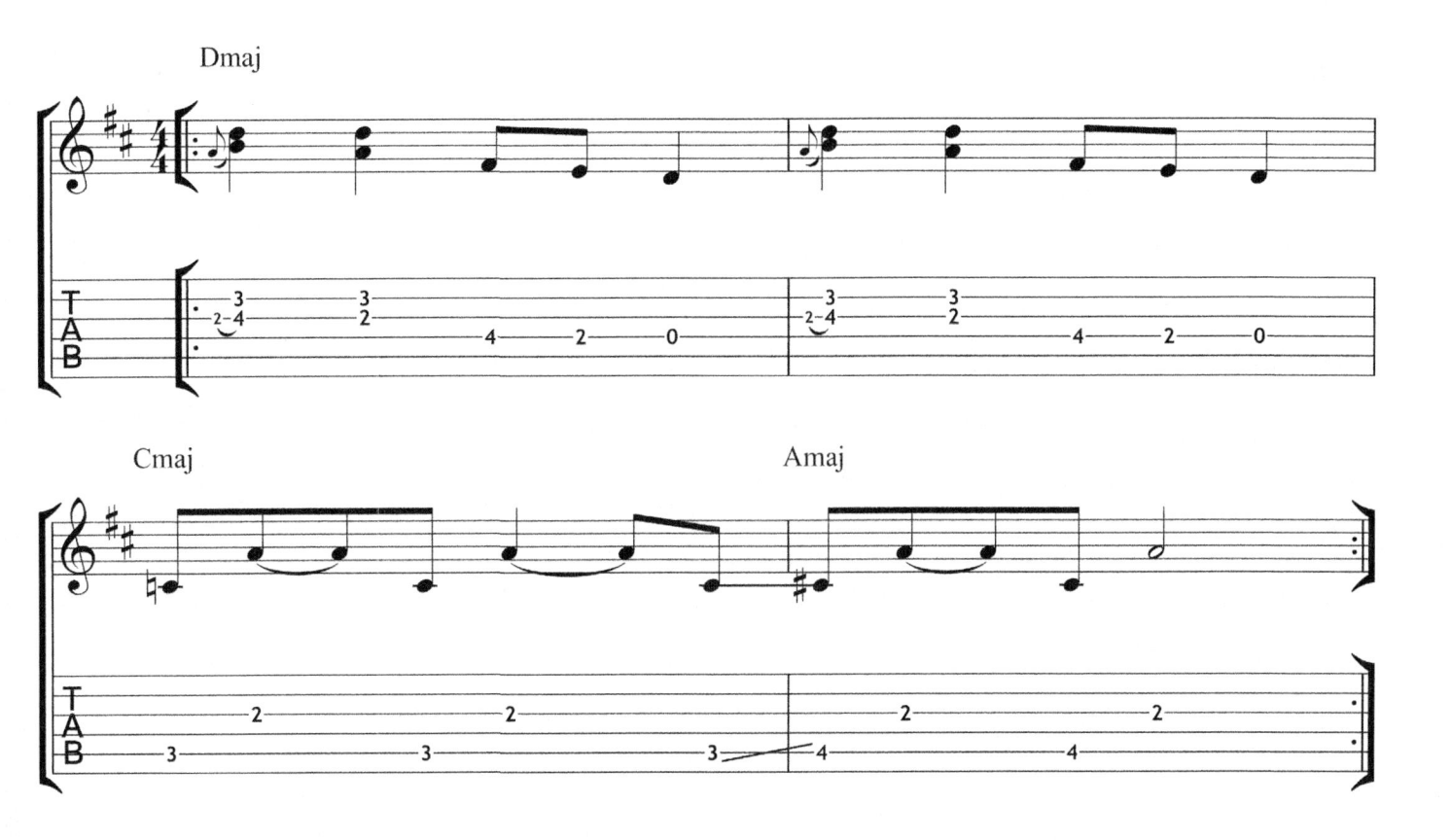

This example shows how Bernie will move from scale-based ideas to more focused chord tone targeting. The country-esque lick in bars 1-2 is based around the D Major Pentatonic scale, while in bar three the C major chord is outlined with root and 5th intervals.

Example 6s

Bernie's banjo playing informs his guitar style, and this example builds a solo from chord shapes, like a banjo player would. The challenge here is the leaps between notes in the first two bars. There are three ways to play this – you can crosspick it with the plectrum, play it totally fingerstyle, or hybrid pick it. For the latter, the pick would play the open D string while the middle finger plays everything else.

Example 6t

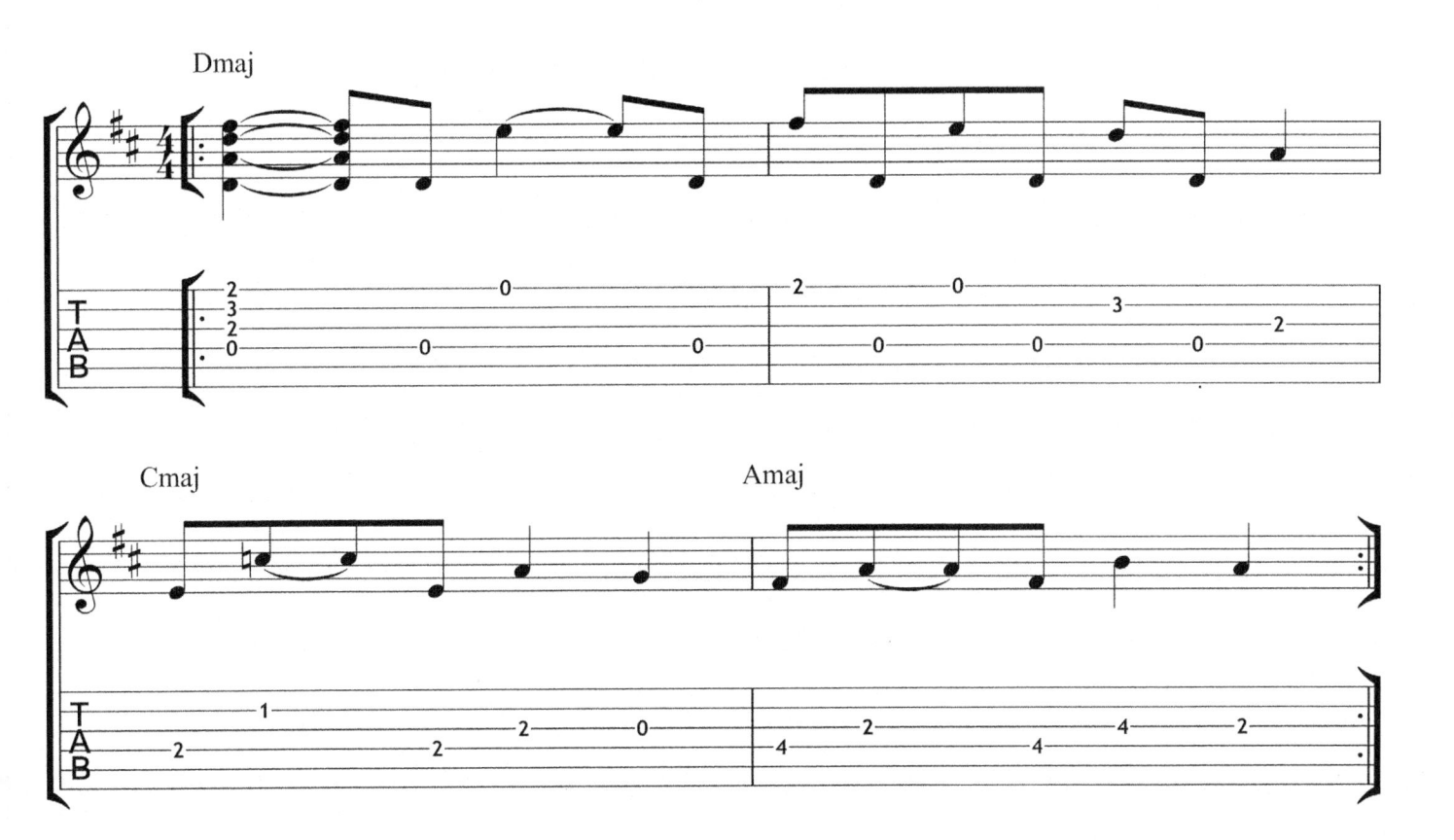

John Fogerty

A legend in the world of country rock, John Fogerty founded Creedence Clearwater Revival and served as the group's vocalist, lead guitarist and principal songwriter. Classics like *Proud Mary*, *Fortunate Son* and *Bad Moon Rising* still receive global airplay today and were instrumental in shaping the country rock sound.

Fogerty's funky riffs and Bayou sound lie at the heart of Creedence Clearwater Revival's music. In this example, bar one shows how Fogerty can build swaggering riffs using the blues scale (E Blues, in this case) while at other times simply highlighting the sound of the dominant 7 chord, as in bar two.

Example 6u

Fogerty fills out his licks with double-stops to great effect, as in this example. This idea is all about the feel that is created, so play it with plenty of attack.

Example 6v

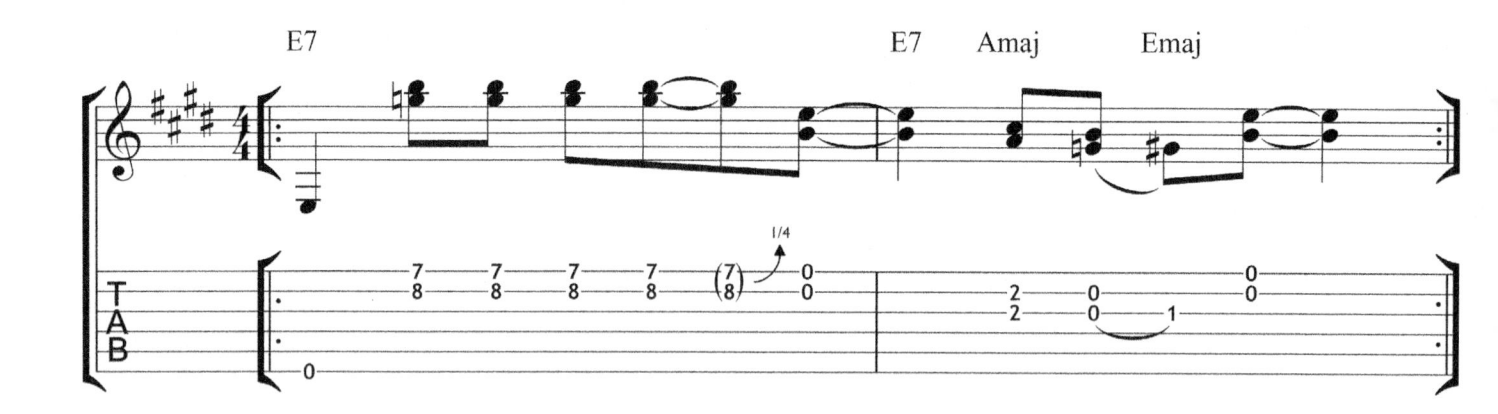

Sometimes simply playing a scale with judicious phrasing results in a lick, as is the case here. This is a Fogerty-inspired run down the E Minor Pentatonic scale, but placing a subtle bend on one or two notes adds character and prevents it from sounding like a scale exercise.

Example 6w

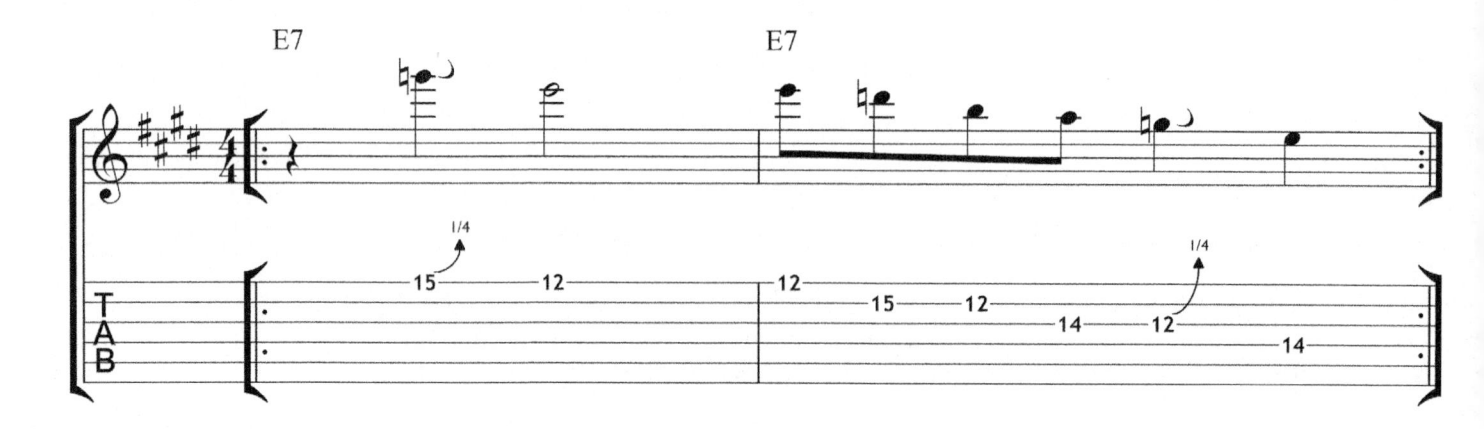

Here's another double-stop line that yields a bluesy sound. Fogerty often takes a less-is-more approach in his playing and the lazy, laid-back feel he achieves is a great thing to aim for. Add a slight bend to both double-stop notes at the end of bar one to create that funky blues sound.

Example 6x

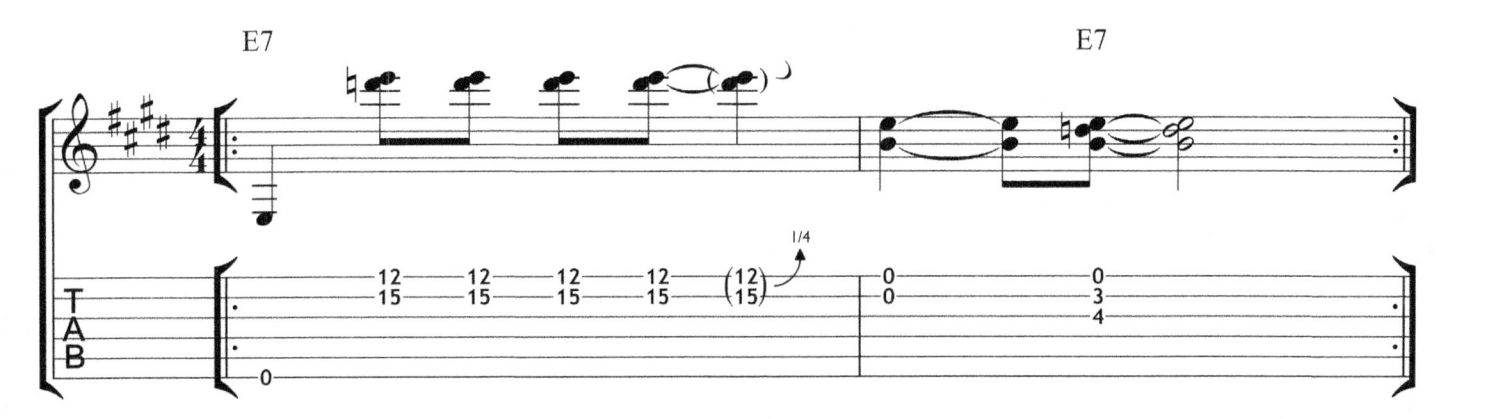

```
        E7                                              E7
     |12---12---12---12---(12)~1/4    0---------0---
     |15---15---15---15---(15)        0---------3---
     |                                          4---
     |0
```

Keith Richards and Mick Taylor

The Rolling Stones may have started life as a British "blues boom" band, but country music has always been close to Keith Richards' heart, with one of his heroes being country star Merle Haggard. When Keith Richards became friends with "outlaw country" legend Gram Parsons, the influence of this genre on the Stones' sound was cemented. Country rock runs through the classic Stones albums *Exile on Main Street* and *Sticky Fingers* via tracks like *Wild Horses* and *Torn and Frayed*.

Keith Richards removes the 6th string from his Telecaster and tunes to open G major (from low to high, D G D G B D). However, it's possible to approximate his approach with standard tuning using triads combined with low open strings.

Bar one of this idea features a classic Keith move: barre the first finger across the 2nd fret, then add the second finger on the B string, 3rd fret, and the third finger on the D string, 4th fret.

Example 6y

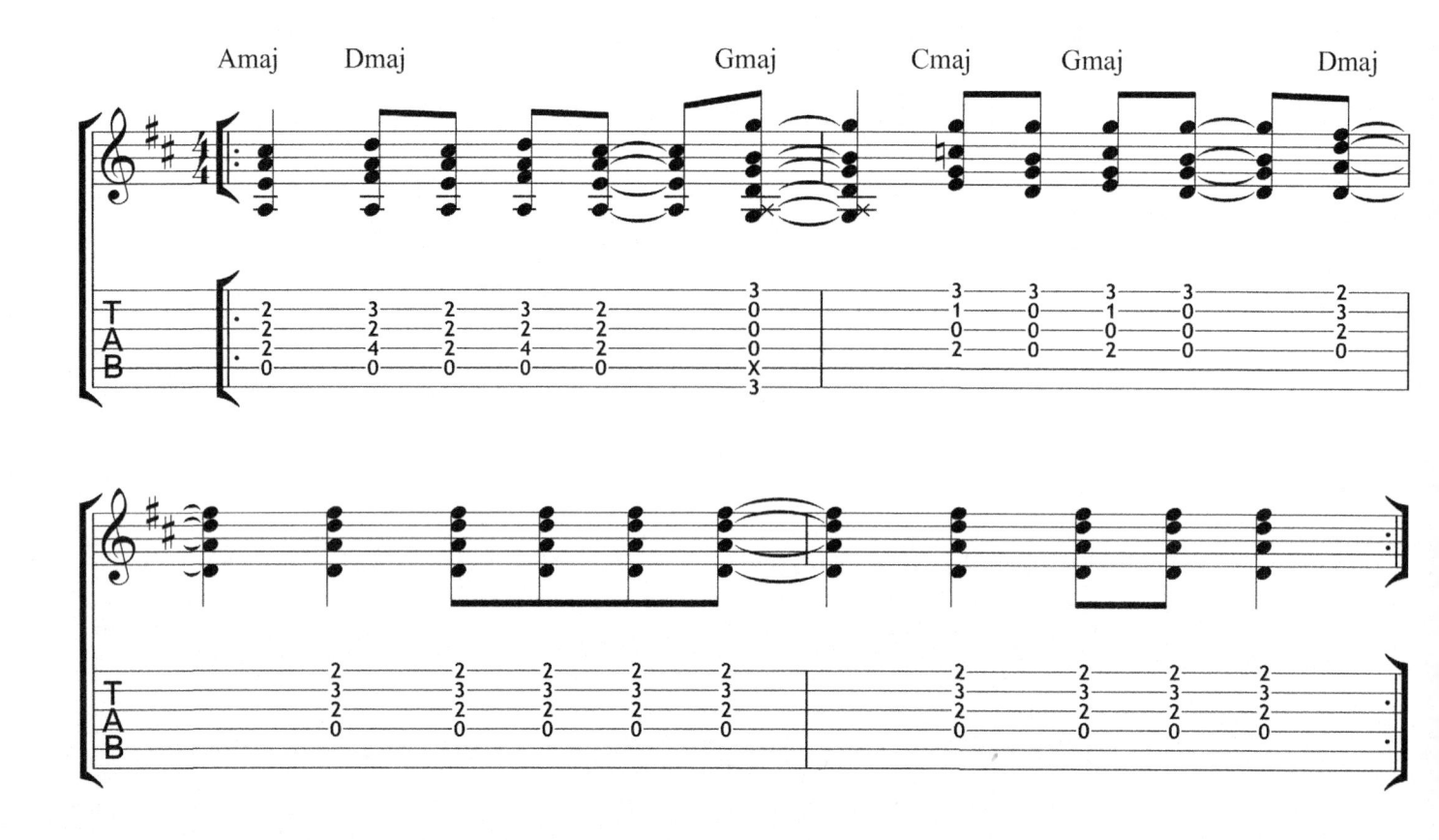

Mick Taylor's country-inspired licks are peppered throughout classic Stones tracks. This idea begins with a chord tone approach before moving to a country lick in bar three. Use the 3rd finger to bend on the G string followed by the 4th finger on the B string and the 1st finger on the 7th fret, E string.

Example 6z

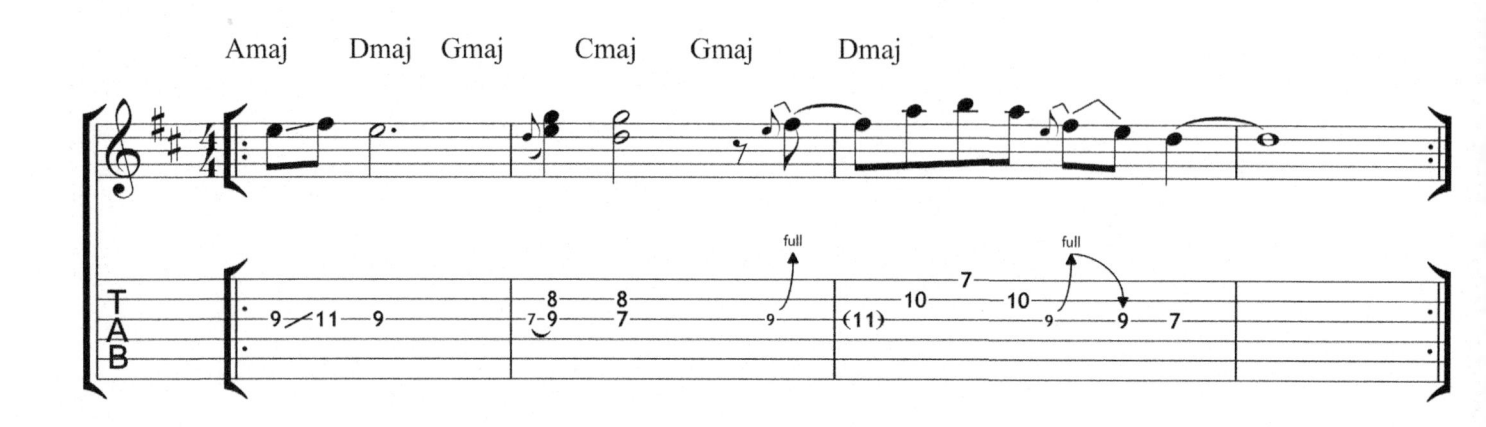

Pedal steel bends are at the heart of this phrase as you put into practice ideas you studied in the earlier chapters on string bending. The key feature is the interplay between the 3rd and 4th fingers on the fretting hand - the 3rd finger takes care of the bend on the G string whilst the 4th finger is simultaneously fretted at the 12th fret of the E string. The lick in Bar three demonstrates how the D Major pentatonic scale (D, E, F#, A, B) can be turned into a musical phrase.

Example 6z1

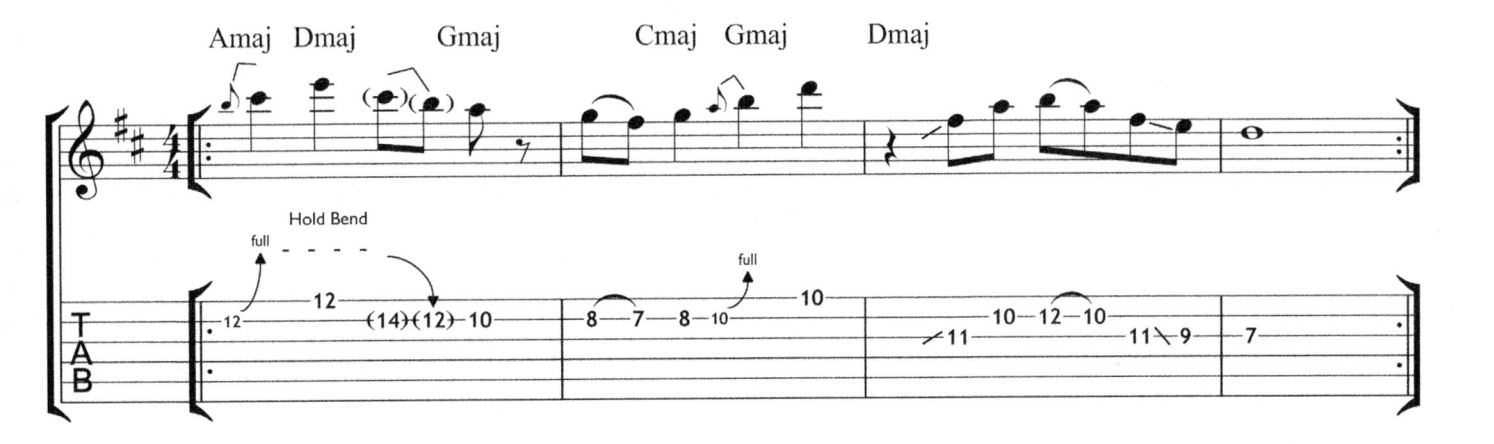

This Mick Taylor style line features some great rhythmic symmetry between the two licks. Start both these licks with the fourth finger of the fretting hand, with the third finger taking care of the bends.

Example 6z2

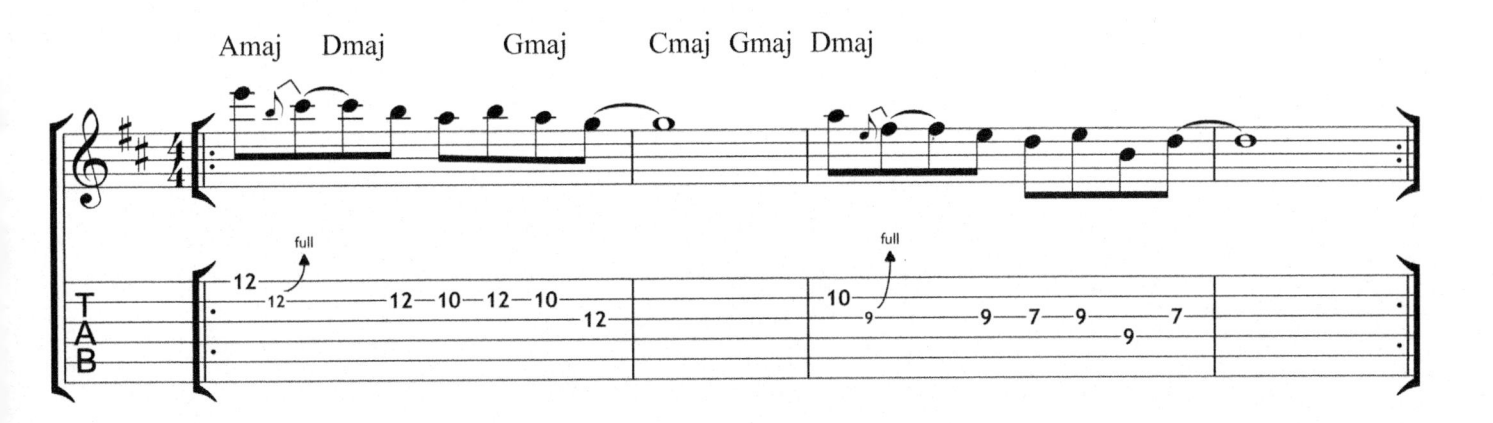

Chapter Seven – Performance Pieces

We round off our exploration of country rock guitar style with four full-length performance pieces that showcase the ideas we've looked at in this book.

Performance piece 1

The first piece is inspired by the country rock sound of Lynyrd Skynyrd, where the guitar plays a detailed part around an underlying chord progression. It's common in this style to have short licks (almost solos) peppered throughout the track. Essentially, wherever the vocals leave some space, the guitar jumps in. You can think of this as a combined rhythm/lead approach, where you constantly veer between these two elements. Of course, the challenge is to make it all flow.

In this piece you'll find crosspicking technique, plenty of string bends and a solo that spans the range of the neck.

The opening phrase features some challenging picking across the strings, so consider what approach will work best for you: crosspicking, hybrid or even fingerpicking.

From bar nine, you'll notice some open chords that avoid using any notes on the A string. From a practical point of view, it's good to use chord voicings that contain fewer notes, as this frees up the fingers to jump between chords and licks more easily. It also prevents the guitar part from muddying up the mix.

From bar fifteen you'll explore the chord/lick approach in more depth before moving on to the solo that begins at bar twenty-three.

The solo is based on the G Major Pentatonic scale (G A B D E) and coves all registers of the neck. The linear approach of moving up the neck highlights how useful it is to know scales all over the fretboard. This knowledge can help you to create solos that build from low to high, taking the listener on a journey.

As well as testing out some of the country rock techniques you've learned, this solo features a ton of classic licks. Memorise them, transpose them to other keys, and remember to use them at the next country rock jam!

Example 7a

13
Gmaj
Cmaj
Cmaj
Gmaj
Gmaj
1/2
16
Gmaj
Fsus2
Cmaj
Gmaj
19
Gmaj
full
Hold Bend
22
Fsus2
Cmaj
Gmaj
TAB

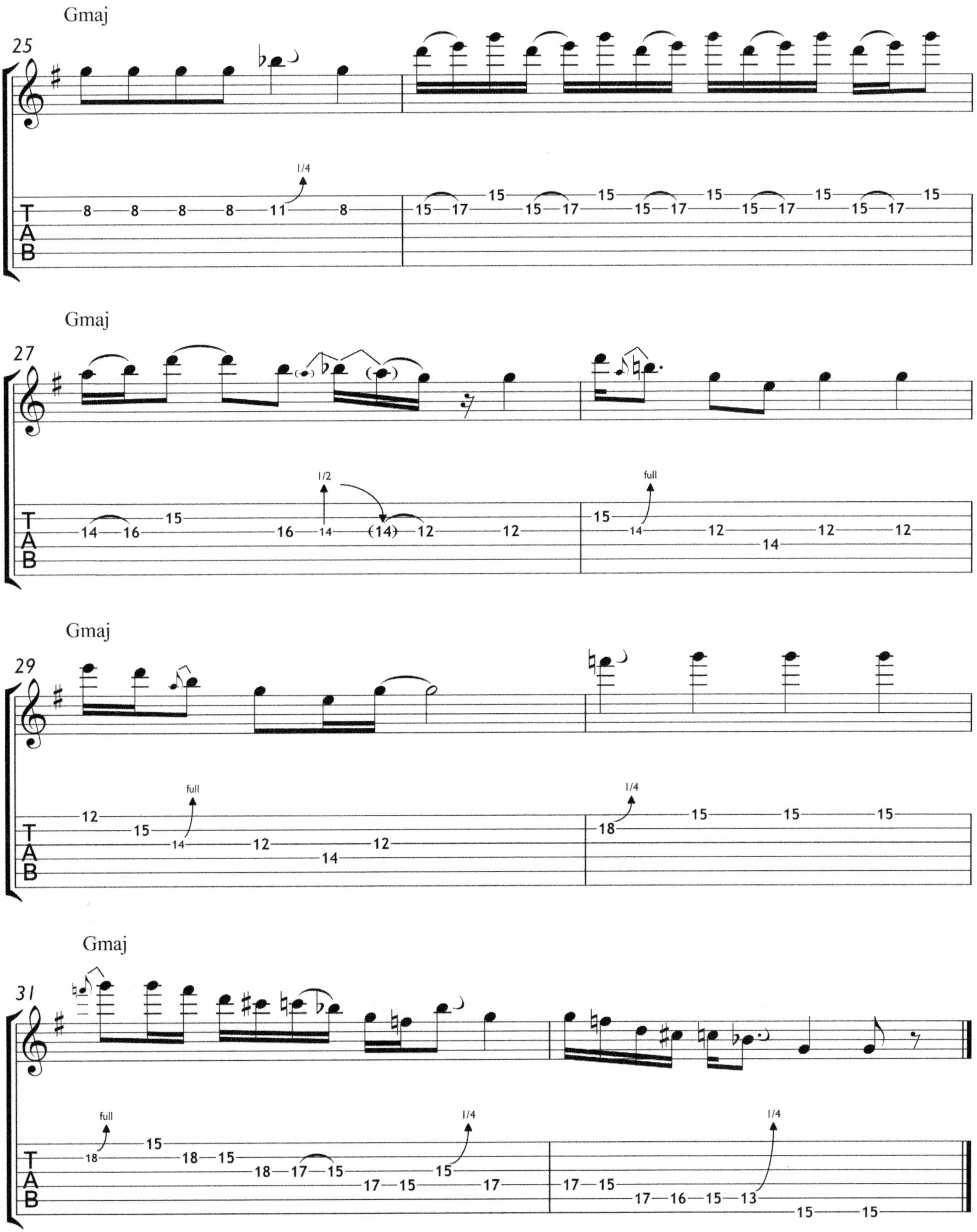
Gmaj
25
1/4
Gmaj
27
1/2
full
Gmaj
29
full
1/4
Gmaj
31
full
1/4
1/4

Performance piece 2

Acoustic guitars have been at the forefront of country rock since the birth of the genre. While the acoustic is often used as a strumming tool to bolster the rhythm section, many players feature it up front and centre, creating complex melodic parts that give a song character. Great examples of this approach are *Wild Horses* and *Anji* by the Rolling Stones, *She Talks to Angels* by The Black Crowes, and *Hotel California* by The Eagles.

This performance piece tips its hat to Keith Richards' approach to acoustic guitar. Instead of simply strumming through the chord progression, the guitar part combines chords with fills, riffs and licks. Everything takes place in the open position, but the challenge is knowing what to play in between each chord. Many of the licks in this piece are staples of the genre, so commit them to memory and they will serve you well in other playing situations where you have to connect similar chords.

When approaching parts like these, assess whether the lick is being played within a chord shape or stands apart from it. For example, in bar two, the phrase after the C major is played within the fingering of the chord, so fretting hand movement is minimal. The same applies to the lick following the Amin7 in bar eleven.

Contrast this with the opening phrase in bar one, which requires more detailed fingering. In this instance, use the second finger for the 4th fret of the G string, followed the first finger on the 3rd fret of the B string. Next, partially barre the 3rd fret of the B and E strings, strike both, then quickly hammer onto the 5th fret, B string with the third finger. Finally, use the second finger to slide down to the 2nd fret, G string, before playing the open G string.

Before playing the whole piece, go through bar by bar and identify those sections that need some forward planning for the fretting hand.

Example 7b

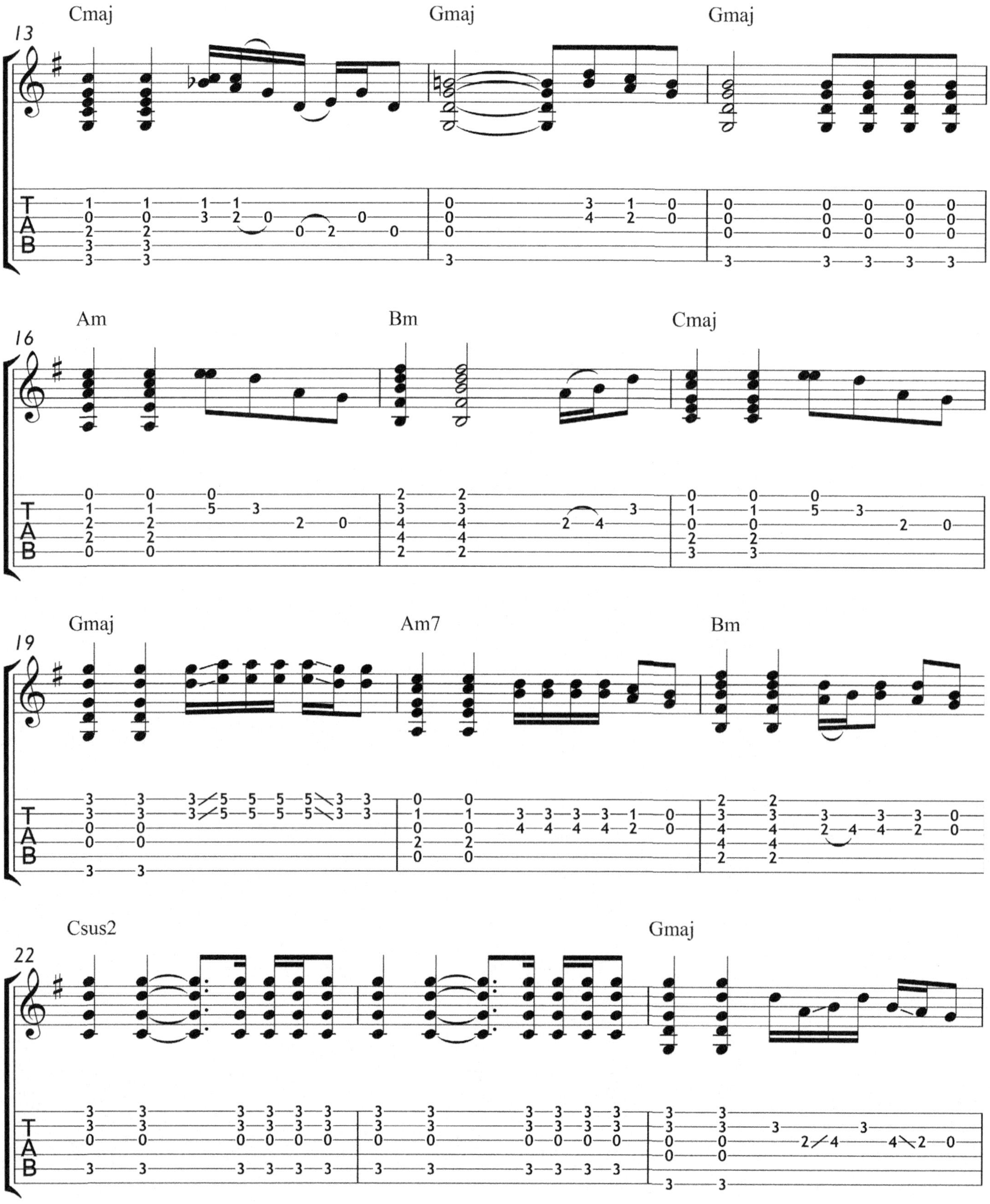
13
Cmaj
Gmaj
Gmaj
16
Am
Bm
Cmaj
19
Gmaj
Am7
Bm
22
Csus2
Gmaj

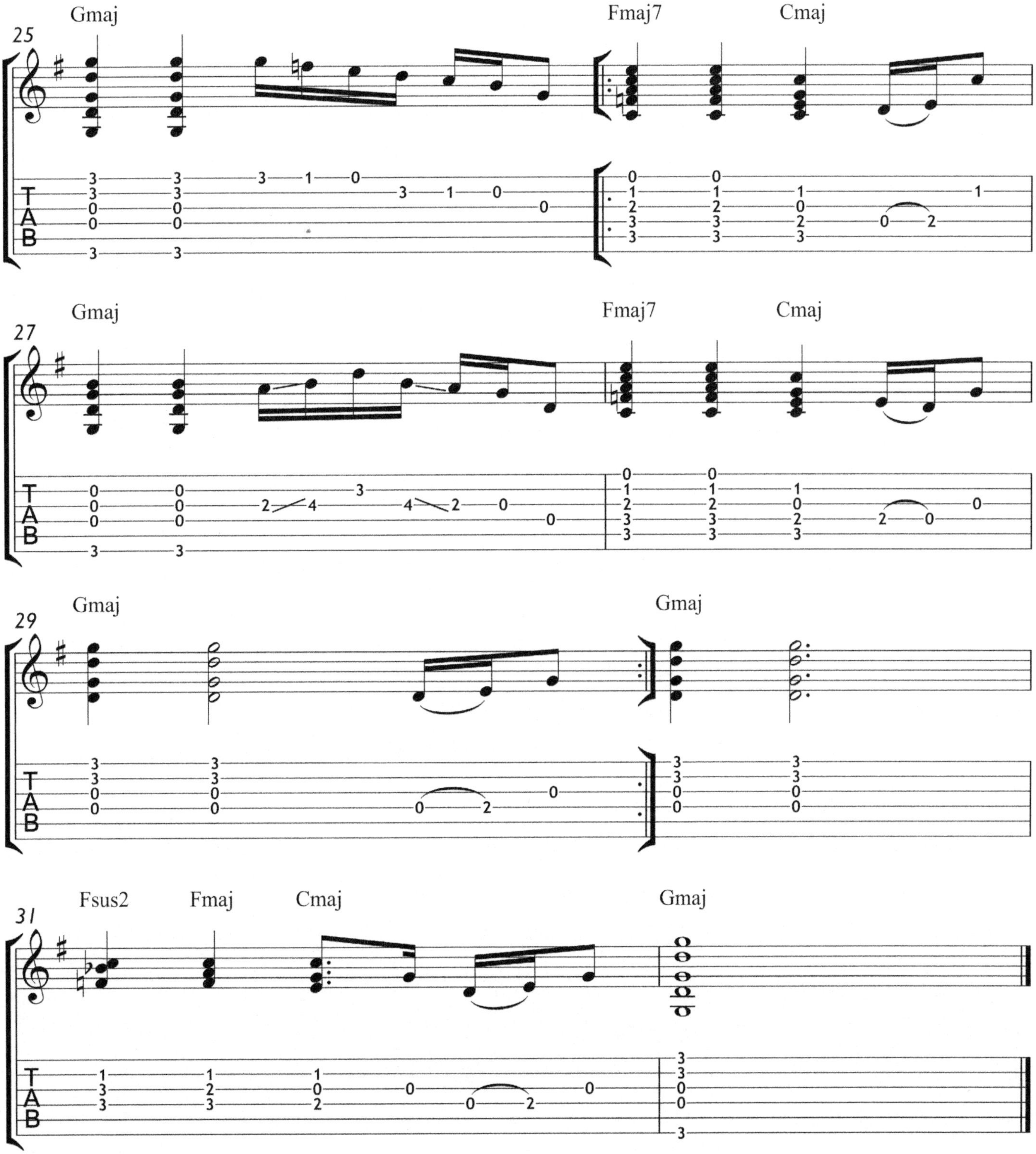
25
Gmaj
Fmaj7
Cmaj
27
Gmaj
Fmaj7
Cmaj
29
Gmaj
Gmaj
31
Fsus2
Fmaj
Cmaj
Gmaj

Performance piece 3

Double-stops and triads are invaluable tools for country rock guitarists. They can be moved around the neck quickly and outline the harmony without making the sound muddy. In bands with two or even three guitarists, it's common for the musicians to divide up the sonic range. Usually, one guitar will take care of parts in the open position/lower register while guitar two is employed to fill things out or to add licks and fills. Alternatively, one guitar might create complementary rhythm parts in the higher register using double-stops/triads.

Eagles legend Joe Walsh frequently uses this approach in his playing. Even before his tenure in The Eagles, he was using double-stop and triad ideas when fronting The James Gang. Joe commonly uses a pedal note, then plays triads against it. This usually means employing an open string, commonly the low E or A, with triads played against it on the D, G and B strings.

You'll see this approach used all the way through this piece. What's even cooler is how easy it is to get creative. Check out the GMaj/A chord in bar seven, for example. Some people would call this an A11 or A9sus4, but in this context it's easier to view it as a simple G major chord over an A pedal tone.

The solo is also inspired by Joe and features some of his classic approaches. It's based around the A Major Pentatonic scale but is given some Joe-esque twists – notably the chromatic lick in bar twenty-four. Chromaticism means injecting notes that don't belong to the key. This creates a brief dissonance that works well as long as you resolve the line to a strong chord tone. In this example, the chromatic phrase on the high E string leads into an A major arpeggio, which is about the safest way you can get out of this lick!

Bar twenty-eight features another Joe-style lick, this time using the concept of motif building. In this case, that means building symmetry within the lick with rhythms that repeat themselves, and the application of bends on the G string. The result is a lick that sounds consistent and cohesive. In short, it's a great way to create a hook within a solo.

Example 7c

10
Amaj Gmaj/A Dmaj/A Amaj A6 A5
12
Amaj Gmaj/A Dmaj/A Amaj Amaj
1/4
14
Amaj Gmaj/A Dmaj/A Amaj A6 A5
16
Amaj Gmaj/A Dmaj/A Amaj A7

18
A7
Emaj
20
Amaj
Hold Bend
1/2
full
full
22
Amaj
full
24
Amaj
full
Hold Bend

26
Amaj
28
Amaj
full
full
full
Hold Bend
30
Amaj
31
Amaj
Hold Bend
1/2

Performance piece 4

Country rock has developed over the years and today, artists like The Black Crowes and Sheryl Crow have found success with their own take on the genre. In some ways, the sound of country rock has softened as it has taken on more of a pop sound, and this performance piece reflects that, focusing more on country rock rhythm guitar than licks and solos.

Players like Peter Stroud (guitarist for Sheryl Crow) are masters of this style. They create solid accompaniment parts that provide a firm foundation for the vocalist to sing over. There are occasional licks and fills, but nothing that will detract from the all-important vocal. The skill is to be able to take a chord progression and move beyond simple strumming to create a guitar part that has plenty of character and interest.

There are various ways to do this and this example achieves it by connecting chords via different inversions. In bar one, for example, the B minor and A major chords are connected via ascending bass notes on the A string.

Another approach is to play arpeggiated chords rather than strumming, which is a great technique for when you want to let the music breathe or create more movement than a simple sustained chord or stab will provide.

Learning how to connect chords with moving bass notes is a great skill to develop. The trick here is to not view every chord in terms of its root note, but to include other chord tones to create an accompaniment. For example, in bar fifteen, the root note of the Cadd9 chord is played, then the 3rd (B) of the G major chord, which neatly connects to the root note of the Bb major chord that follows in bar sixteen.

Example 7d

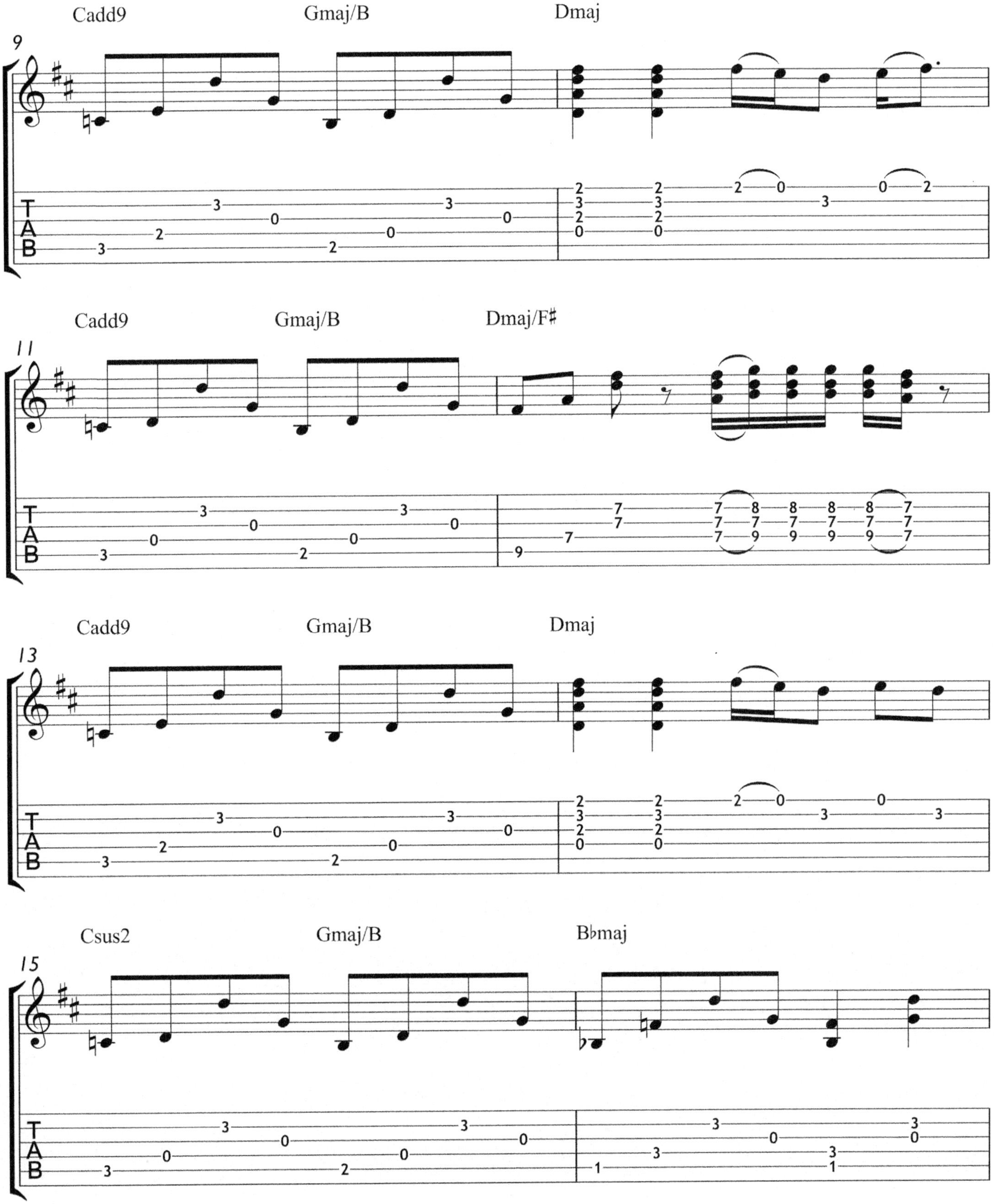
Cadd9
Gmaj/B
Dmaj
9
Cadd9
Gmaj/B
Dmaj/F♯
11
Cadd9
Gmaj/B
Dmaj
13
Csus2
Gmaj/B
B♭maj
15

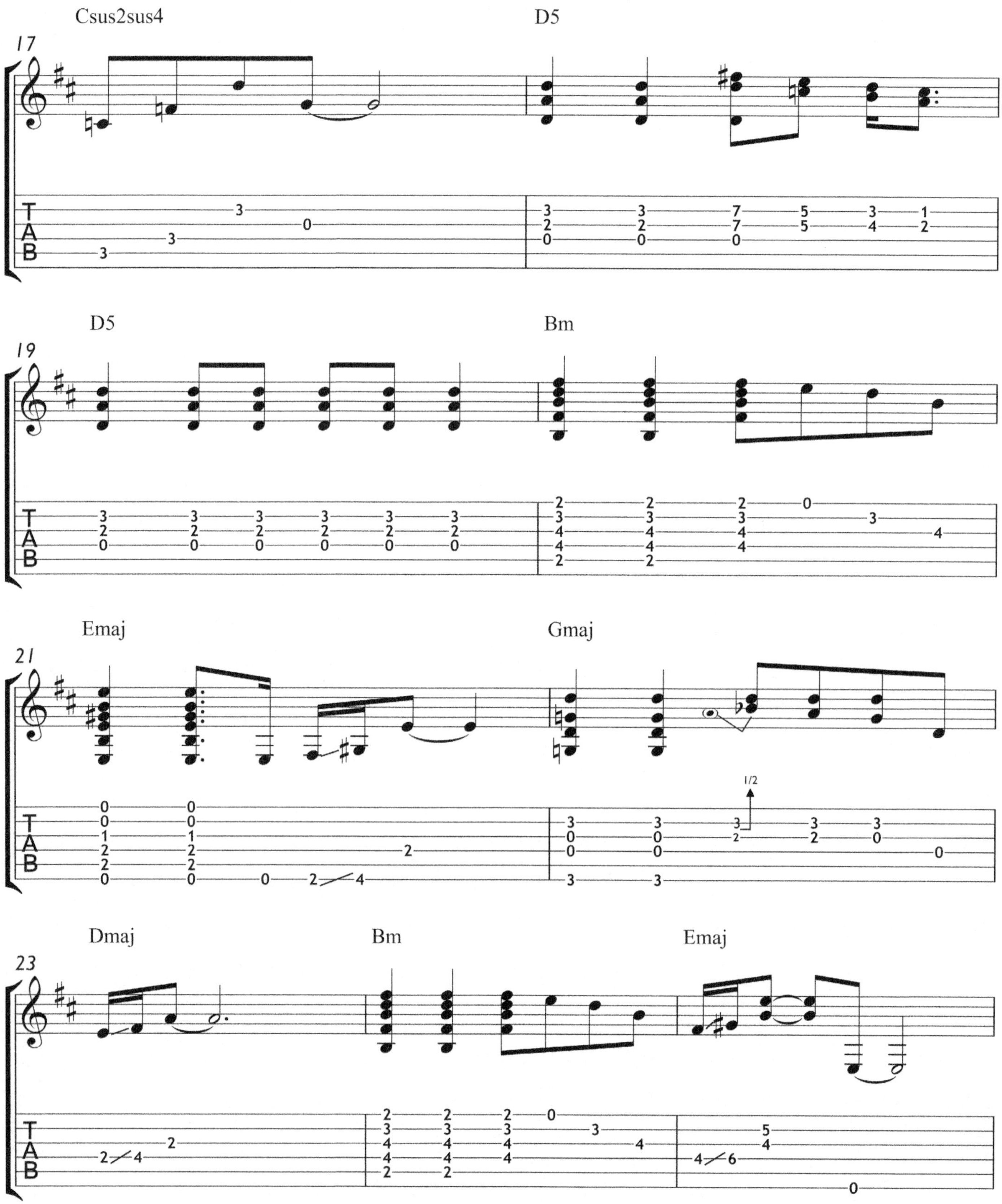
Csus2sus4
D5
D5
Bm
Emaj
Gmaj
Dmaj
Bm
Emaj

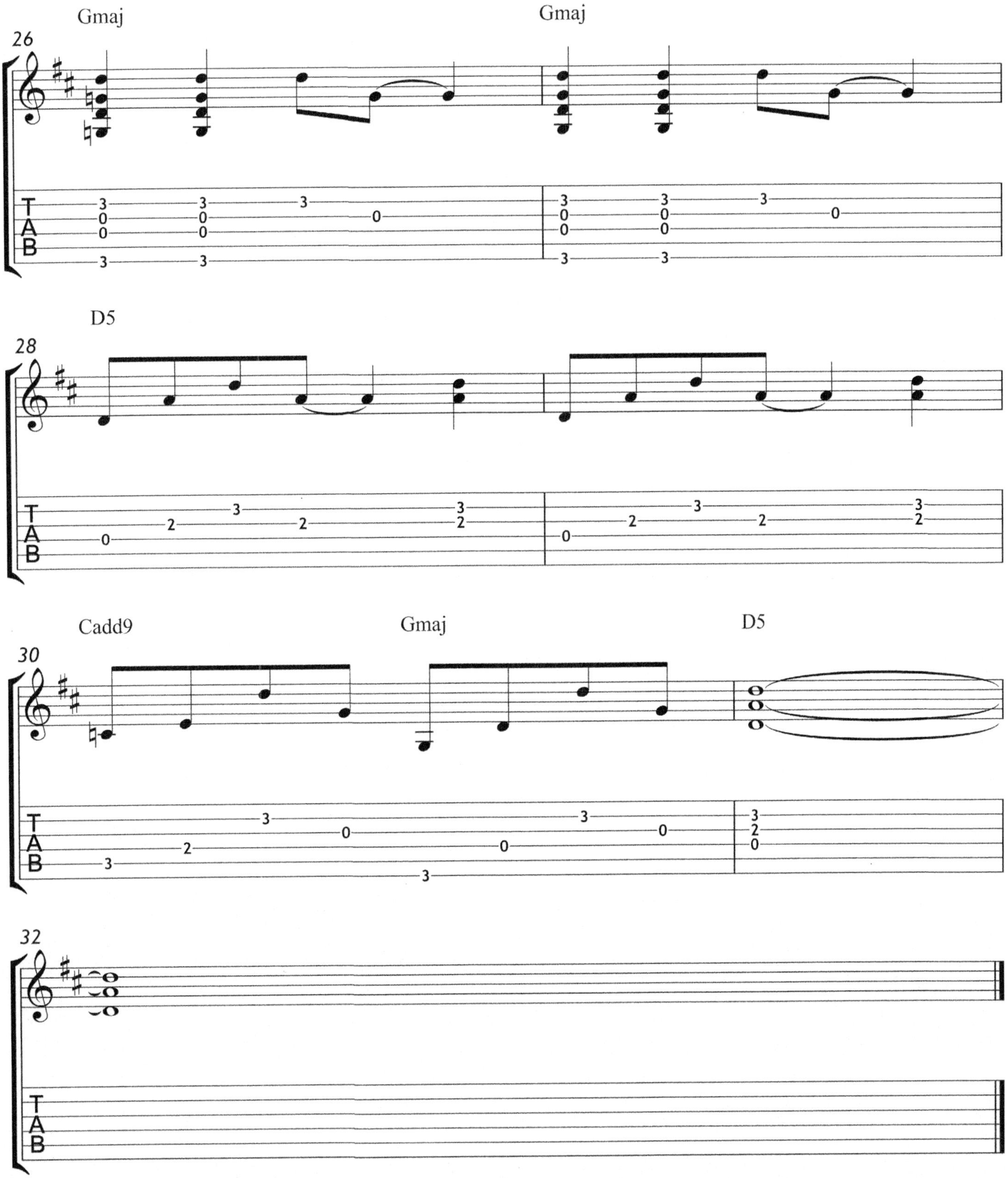
Gmaj
Gmaj
26
D5
28
Cadd9
Gmaj
D5
30
32

Conclusion

Country rock is a broad genre that provides a rich seam of learning for guitarists from any style. The fusing together of the worlds of country and rock music created a unique sound that allowed for many variations, from the southern rock scene to the softer Laurel Canyon sound of LA.

When you have mastered the material in this book, try broadening your listening (and learning) to include other seminal country rock bands like Poco and The Marshall Tucker Band. The more you listen to classic rock, the more you'll hear elements of country rock in there too. Think of how country rock helped shape the sound of bands like Tom Petty and The Heartbreakers and elements of James Taylor's style.

Country rock has never been stronger and today artists like Jason Isbell, The Black Crowes, Sheryl Crow and Chris Stapleton take elements of the genre and mix it with classic country, rock and Americana to develop their own unique sounds.

Don't be afraid to take the techniques and licks you have learned here into other styles. Hybrid picking, country bends and double-stops can all be used in rock, blues, soul and many more genres. The most important thing is to have fun and be adventurous with what you've learned.

Enjoy!

Stu.

Printed in Great Britain
by Amazon